VESTRY REFLECTIONS

Cultivating Spiritual Growth
in Church Leaders

MARC D. SMITH

Copyright © 2025 Marc D. Smith

All rights reserved. No part of this book may be reproduced, stored in a retrieval system, or transmitted in any form or by any means, electronic or mechanical, including photocopying, recording, or otherwise, without the written permission of the publisher.

Unless otherwise noted, Scripture quotations are from The New Revised Standard Version Bible, copyright © 1989 National Council of the Churches of Christ in the United States of America. Used by permission. All rights reserved worldwide.

Scripture quotations marked KJV are taken from the King James Version, public domain.

Church Publishing
19 East 34th Street
New York, NY 10016
www.churchpublishing.org

Cover design by Newgen
Typeset by Nord Compo

ISBN 978-1-64065-780-9 (paperback)
ISBN 978-1-64065-798-4 (eBook)

Library of Congress Control Number: 2025940998

*To the Revs. Lee Joesten,
who first gave me a glimpse of ordained ministry,
and Tim Mueller, who helped me reclaim a faith almost lost,
and the Revs. Harv Sanders, Shariya Molegoda,
and Anne Kelsey, who nurtured my Anglican sensibilities.*

CONTENTS

Introduction vii

Governing Faithfully 1
   The Business of the Church 1
   "Be Thou My Vision" 5
   What Are We Called to Do? 10
   Values Drive Decisions 14
   Beyond Fiduciary Responsibilities 19
   . . . And God Laughs 26

Around the Church 33
   The Servant Who Leads or the Leader Who Serves? 33
   What Makes Space Sacred? 39
   The Work of the People 44
   Giving Voice to Our Faith 51
   Put Your Money Where Your Faith Is 60
   Channeling Our Best Intentions 64
   Violence in Our Midst 72
   When Things "Go off the Rails" 79
   Clergy Taking Leave 84
   "Peace"—Welcoming Clergy 88

Nurturing the Soul 95
   Where It All Began: Knitting Our "Ahas" Together 95
   Making Disciples: Bringing Christ to the World 101
   Faith Seeking Understanding 107
   Abundance in the Face of Scarcity 112
   Catch Your Breath . . . But Hold on to Your Seat 119
   Be Still 124
   On Bended Knee 130
   "No Man Is an Island" 136
   "Do Not Be Afraid" 142
   "Why Have You Forsaken Me?" 149

Faith's Journey Throughout the Year 157
    Advent's Question: How Could This Be? 157
    "In the Beginning Was the Word": Christmas' Proclamation . . . 162
    Lost in Epiphany's Shuffle 168
    Lent's Call: Seeking and Sharing Forgiveness 174
    Easter's Challenge. 180
    The Voice of Pentecost 185
    Creation: Celebration and Care 190

Closing Prayer 197

References 199

Acknowledgments 209

INTRODUCTION

I recall fondly the discernment retreats I attended throughout my formation for the priesthood in the Episcopal Diocese of Missouri. Without fail, the question was always posed to Bishop Wayne Smith, "What are you looking for in prospective priests?" During these times of reflection with participants in various stages of discernment and formation, his response was always the same: "It's not what I'm looking for but what the Church needs—and that's leaders." I found this especially affirming since I was wrapping up a successful 35-year career in the leadership of academic- and community-based health-care organizations. And since my youth, I had regularly found myself in a variety of leadership roles in professional, civic, and religious organizations. "How can I miss?" I thought, as I assessed my prospects for ordination. But like most things in the discernment process, this was to take an interesting turn.

I'm not conscious of ever flaunting my leadership, elevating the trappings that often accompany it or too frequently believing my own publicity. Nevertheless, my rector at Grace Episcopal Church in Jefferson City, Missouri, the since retired Rev. Harv Sanders, recognized the potential pitfall of assuming that my secular experience would readily transfer to the life of the Church without first examining it.

So, he challenged me in the fall of 2005 to reflect on the specific nature of leadership in communities of faith and summarize my thoughts in a paper we could discuss together.

To this day, I remain deeply indebted to Harv for his foresight, encouragement, and mentoring.

Since this exercise two decades ago, I've continued to explore the concept of leadership in congregational life, focusing particularly on the role of vestries and their clergy partners. *Vestry Reflections: Cultivating Spiritual Growth in Church Leaders* reflects my study, thinking, and experience. Although I've certainly evolved in my approach to leadership, the concepts shared with Harv—although by no means exhaustive—still ground my ministry and frame this book.

Central to the faithful exercise of leadership in the context of the life we share in community is the acceptance of it as a "call." It's not a job or a profession or a rank. Rather, it's God's invitation to and acceptance of a particular form of discipleship, as beautifully articulated by Thomas Merton (2007):

> Many poets are not poets for the same reason that many religious men are not saints: they never succeed in being themselves. They never get around to being the particular poet or the particular monk they are intended to be by God. They never become the man or the artist who is called for by all the circumstances of their individual lives.

Leadership requires not only strategic and operational skill but, most important, the ability to shape and articulate a congregation's vision, mission, and values and consistently ground decisions in them. The author of the Book of Proverbs understood this well, noting that "Where there is no vision, the people perish" (Proverbs 29.18 KJV).

Perhaps the most frequently ignored dimension of leadership is the capacity to listen—not merely to refrain from speaking but the willingness to hear the unfamiliar, the unwanted, and the uncomfortable, to comprehend their potential and to translate their meaning for the congregation. And it recognizes that the ongoing spiritual formation of the Church is iterative, constantly reshaping all those who hear and experience the witness of Christ. Again, the Book of Proverbs provides sound advice, stating "the ear of the wise seeks knowledge" (18.15b).

Inspiration—the ability to help organizations and those who serve in them achieve goals they may not have imagined attainable—also is an essential quality of effective leadership. In addition, it necessitates prudent risk-taking, as boldly declared by President Theodore Roosevelt:

> Far better it is to dare mighty things, to win glorious triumphs, even though checkered by failure, than to take rank with those poor spirits who neither enjoy much or suffer much, because they live the gray twilight that knows not victory nor defeat.

Leadership is a communal activity that begins with and is given legitimacy by the congregation. Although position and title may facilitate it, leadership fundamentally flows from the search for purpose and direction by parishioners and staff alike. It's conferred by the group, not assumed by the individual, and, as shared by Henri Nouwen, "can only be honest if it takes the form of service" (1977).

Finally, St. Benedict of Nursia provides a pointed reminder of the critical importance of accountability in leadership:

"The prioress and abbot must always remember what they are and remember what they are called, aware that more will be expected of one to whom more has been entrusted" (1997). For the servant leader, accountability is much more than the mere recognition that "the buck stops here." It requires a genuine and humble assessment of self, as well as a style that is just, cohesive, consistent, and grounded in trust.

My prayerful hope is that this modest work will stimulate even deeper reflection on the relationship between parish governance and spiritual growth. May God bless your ministry with wisdom, a compassionate heart, and a generous spirit.

The Rev. Marc D. Smith, Ph.D.
Epiphany 2025

GOVERNING FAITHFULLY

The Business of the Church

Opening Prayer

God of unlimited possibilities, grace us with your Spirit as we discern our ministry and together define our work in a world of complexity, competing priorities, and uncertainty. Open our hearts and minds that we might share your vision for a world truly and fully at peace. Open our eyes and ears that we may know the needs of the most vulnerable among us. And open our hands that we might serve them—humbly, faithfully, and lovingly. Amen.

A Quote for Your Consideration

Opportunities to pursue new ministries and the need to discontinue others, the uncertainty of a congregation's future, the priorities to be embraced, and the specific work to be done regularly challenge vestries. Twentieth-century Episcopal champion of lay leadership Verna Dozier provides wise counsel and clear direction for clergy and vestries (2002):

> What is the church's business? ... Not soul saving. God has already done that, and nothing can be added

to God's almighty work. Not legislating morality. That's shifty sand and lures us away from the biblical call to repent. Not social service. The need for the church to do social service is eloquent testimony, to me, that we have failed in our business. So what is our business? Ministry.

Leadership in Context

"Ministry?" How easy it is for us to be confused by the call to proclaim the Gospel, the work to be done, and the authority under which we serve. For many of us, our thoughts about ministry are largely (if not completely) embedded in the lives of those ordained to it. After all, they preach, teach, and administer the Sacraments—each fundamental to communities of faith. Still others ascribe "ministry" to virtually anything done in or by a church in furthering its presence among congregants and in the life of the world. And finally, a significant number of us hold to the doctrine of the "priesthood of all believers" without seriously exploring its personal and communal implications.

If we accept Dozier's assertion that the "business" of the church is ministry (and I think we should), then it's incumbent on vestry leaders to understand its many facets and how they can be integrated to support their congregation and serve the larger community. Anglican theologian Paul Avis (2000) proffers three principles for both lay and ordained ministry. First, ministry is the work of Jesus Christ through human actions guided by the Holy Spirit. Second, baptism is the foundation for all ministry. And third, ministry reflects the common beliefs, values, and actions of a congregation in its shared life, as well as in its interaction with the world around it. Clear in Avis' formulation is that the recognition of ministry among the entire Body of Christ—lay and clergy alike—embodies who we are, the gifts we've been given, and the way they're used.

St. Paul's Letter to the Romans not only provides the foundation for Avis' concept of ministry but also illustrates it:

> For as in one body we have many members, and not all the members have the same function, so we, who are many, are one body in Christ, and individually we are members one of another. We have gifts that differ according to the grace given to us: prophecy, in proportion to faith; ministry, in ministering; the teacher, in teaching; the exhorter, in exhortation; the giver, in generosity; the leader, in diligence; the compassionate, in cheerfulness (Romans 12.4–8).

Thus, we understand that ministry is reflected in many different gifts distributed across the entire Church. But the mere receipt of God's gifts, regardless of their bounty or diversity, is not sufficient for ministry as the Body of Christ. Rather, Paul punctuates the absolute necessity for all that has been gifted to us through the Holy Spirit to be accomplished in our care of each other and the world:

> Let love be genuine; hate what is evil, hold fast to what is good; love one another with mutual affection; outdo one another in showing honor. Do not lag in zeal, be ardent in spirit, serve the Lord. Rejoice

in hope, be patient in suffering, persevere in prayer. Contribute to the needs of the saints; extend hospitality to strangers (Romans 12.9–13).

The implications of this understanding of ministry for vestries and other congregational leaders are several. Most important, we're challenged to assist each member of our community in discerning their gifts for ministry and encouraging their use. In addition, discovering and defining ministries fully grounded in our baptismal life—whether internally or beyond the walls of our sanctuary—are essential to focusing this work and legitimizing it as an extension of Jesus' presence. Finally, and of no less consequence for the governance of the congregation, is the necessity to defer whenever possible to lay or mutual ministry, reserving for the clergy those ministries which only they've been ordained to conduct or for which they have a particularly special gift. Not only will this diminish the potential for clericalism—real or perceived—but it will allow everyone's gifts for ministry to flourish and be distributed across the congregation in a proportional way.

Vestry Discussion

- How does Dozier's perspective on ministry—what it is and what it isn't—affect your sense of the challenges your congregation is confronting and how you might address them?
- What is the vestry's specific role in identifying and nurturing appropriate ministries within the

congregation, as well as limiting or failing to endorse others?

- What are your gifts for ministry, and are you using them fully? If not, why, and what might be done to overcome impediments?

Something to Ponder

No organization, including a church, is capable of "being all things to all people." In fact, attempting this is a sure path to a lack of focus, burnout, and frustration—if not failure. Setting our priorities together, we can reasonably and responsibly aspire to ministries within our reach that in some way touch each member of the congregation and enrich the life of the entire community. Therefore, you're encouraged to reflect on the concept of "priorities" in the context of the leadership of your parish.

"Be Thou My Vision"

Opening Prayer

O God, whose mind envisioned a world made perfect and created it as an expression of the Divine: open our eyes to see and embrace all that God would have for us; unmask our blindness to the needs of a fractured world; and send your Holy Spirit to encourage us, support us, and give us hope as Your Kingdom unfolds. For the sake of your Son, Jesus Christ, we pray. Amen.

A *Quote for Your Consideration*

The late president of the University of Notre Dame, the Rev. Theodore Hesburgh, famously observed, "You can't blow an uncertain trumpet." The certainty of a congregation's "vision" (or that of any other organization, for that matter) is essential for understanding, interpreting, and living in the ministry to which it has been called and the work it's to do. Vestries and their clergy partners are regularly challenged by complex issues and difficult decisions. Crafting a truly aspirational vision with broad congregational participation in the process and consistently using it to guide your work is fundamental to ensuring a healthy, vibrant, and focused community of faith. This hope for clarity and Divine guidance is beautifully expressed in the prayerful Episcopal hymn "Be Thou My Vision" (1982):

> Be thou my vision, O Lord of my heart;
> All else be nought to me, save that thou art—
> Thou my best thought, by day or by night,
> Waking or sleeping, thy presence my light.

> Be thou my wisdom, and thou my true word;
> I ever with thee and thou with me, Lord;
> Thou my great Father; thine own may I be;
> Thou in me dwelling, and I one with thee.

> High King of heaven, when victory is won,
> May I reach heaven's joys, bright heaven's Sun!
> Heart of my heart, whatever befall,
> Still be my vision, O Ruler of all.

Leadership in Context

Corporate theorists, management consultants, and strategy gurus have long debated the definitions of *organizational vision*, *mission*, and *values*. Without wading into that contentious quagmire, this discussion assumes that *vision* defines the ideal environment to which a church aspires. So, for example, a congregation might express a vision "that all within our community experience the grace of God and the Good News of the Gospel of Jesus Christ."

Clearly, this illustration is aspirational, reflecting a state of the community that can never be fully achieved. Nevertheless, it provides a destination for the parish's journey of faith and a focus for ministry. Absent a clear vision for the future, no church can ultimately succeed.

The Book of Proverbs punctuates just this point: "Where there is no vision, the people perish" (Prov. 29.18, KJV). Positioned in the subsection of the book focused on the obligations of rulers who are responsible for ensuring justice, the author proffers a vision for a society faithful to the Torah and receptive to God's ongoing presence revealed through the prophets. Although Proverbs appears relatively late in the canon of Hebrew Scriptures, the importance of "vision" is present from the moment of Creation.

In the beginning when God created the heavens and the earth, the earth was formless and void and darkness covered the face of the deep, while a wind from God swept over the face of the waters ... God saw everything that he had made, and indeed, it was very good" (Genesis 1.1–2, 31a).

Out of nothing, God created all that exists and brought a distinct order to what could have been chaos. The text is quite clear that God did not simply roll out matter and let it become whatever it might. Rather, there was an expressed, clear, and decisive intent to Creation—a vision for what would come.

Likewise, God's vision for the future is captured in the covenant forged with Abram:

> Now the Lord said to Abram, "Go from your country and your kindred and your father's house to the land that I will show you. I will make of you a great nation, and I will bless you and make your name great, so that you will be a blessing. I will bless those who bless you, and the one who curses you I will curse; and in you all the families of the earth shall be blessed" (Genesis 12.1–3).

And as the destination of Scripture's salvation narrative, Jesus shares his vision for God's faithful:

> In my Father's house there are many dwelling places. If it were not so, would I have told you that I go to prepare a place for you? And if I go to prepare a place for you, I will come again and take you to myself, so that where I am, there you may be also. And you know the way to the place where I am going." Thomas said to him, "Lord, we do not know where you are going. How can we know the way?" Jesus said to him, "I am the way and the truth and the life. No one comes to the Father except through me. If you know me, you

will know my Father also. From now on you do know him and have seen him" (John 14.2–7).

Whether in God's commitments over millennia or the lofty aspirations of today's faith communities, vision enables us to see the destination of our journey, anticipate the experience of arriving at it, and assess our progress along the way. Empowered by the Holy Spirit, vision also functions as an active enabler, lifting and encouraging us on our path. As so lovingly expressed by the author of "Be Thou My Vision," we implore God to live in our hearts, be our best thought and the source of wisdom, and remain ever-present dwelling in us as one—all that we might attain God's vision for us. "May I reach heaven's joys, bright heaven's Sun!"

Vestry Discussion

- Does your congregation have a clear, concise, and memorable vision?
- How do you use your vision in guiding the work of the vestry and setting priorities for ministry?
- How does this vision shape your personal spiritual journey and the work you're called to do?

Something to Ponder

The concept of "vision" describes a state that often will never be achieved—a world free of war, a community without disease, or a neighborhood in which crime has totally been eradicated, for example. Nevertheless, we continue to pursue it hoping at least to make progress. Therefore, you're invited to reflect on the word *strive* as you consider your congregation's vision.

What Are We Called to Do?

Opening Prayer

God of unbounded embrace and love, we pray especially for all whose lives have been diminished by the heritage of their birth, the tint of their skin, the opportunity for work, their access to shelter, food, and health care, and the simple respect due equal members of our human family. Bless the work we do to enact the Gospel of Jesus Christ in our care of the world and the most vulnerable among us. In Jesus' Name we pray. Amen.

A Quote for Your Consideration

Setting priorities among the many ministries a congregation might embrace is an essential function of the vestry. The process requires a substantive understanding of them, as well as of the parish's mission and capabilities. Most important, it's rooted in our witness to the presence of Christ in our world. You're invited to consider the following quote from sixteenth-century Spanish mystic St. Teresa of Ávila:

> Christ has no body now on earth but yours, no hands but yours, no feet but yours. Yours are the eyes through which to look out Christ's compassion to the world.

Yours are the feet with which he is to go about doing good. Yours are the hands with which he is to bless men now.

Leadership in Context

If *vision* defines the ideal environment to which a church or any organization aspires, then *mission* reflects the distinct (but not necessarily unique) role it has in accomplishing it. So, for example, a local charity might express its vision as "a community in which no one is involuntarily unhoused," while its specific mission could be "to construct tiny homes for the unhoused in our community." Since mission statements are not necessarily exclusive, an entity with the same vision could also have a mission to "advocate for local policy and legislative initiatives to decrease the number of involuntarily unhoused people in our community." The purpose of both vision and mission statements is not to define a unique role but rather to refine and focus the organization's perspective on each, a particular challenge for the Church and its millions of congregations worldwide.

The Gospel of Matthew's "Great Commandment" provides a clear and unambiguous mission for all who would be Jesus' disciples: "Go therefore and make disciples of all nations, baptizing them in the name of the Father and of the Son and of the Holy Spirit, and teaching them to obey everything that I have commanded you" (Matthew 28.19–20a). The "Farewell Discourse" in John's Gospel offers additional guidance for the ministry of the faithful: "This is my [Jesus'] commandment, that you love one another as I have loved you" (John 15.12).

Together, they offer a solid foundation for the work of the Church. We're to proclaim the Good News of His resurrection to the farthest corners of the earth. We're to welcome everyone who believes into the universal Body of Christ through baptism. And we're to reflect the presence of Jesus to the world by extending His unbounded and unequivocal love to all. However, they don't provide the specificity necessary for individual faith communities to chart their future in the detail that's necessary or to determine the resources essential to accomplishing its goals.

Within the broad context of the Church's imperative to evangelize and love fervently, how might an individual congregation and its vestry understand its mission? And how might it fashion a meaningful and actionable mission statement?

Key to discerning a congregation's mission is a shared understanding of its vision. What's the "world" our parish imagines and is prepared to shape? And regardless of the extent that it's reasonably achievable, a church's vision sets the expectation for its ministry. It answers the question: "Where are we going?" To stake out the work before us—our mission—we need to know the destination. A clearly informed and articulated vision is, therefore, the foundation for a congregation's discernment of mission and planning to accomplish it.

Although mission statements are best when they're aspirational, they also need to reflect the realities of the congregation and environment in which they're grounded. Data and qualitative information (however imperfect) about the need the parish intends to address as the focus of its ministry and its capabilities are essential to the process of mission development and articulation. And while the eventual mission statement might be a lengthy stretch for the congregation, it should not be so far removed from real possibilities that it loses its ability to inspire and motivate.

Just as information and data are necessary in establishing a congregation's mission, so too are they critical to the ongoing evaluation of progress in achieving it. The longstanding business adage that "if it's not measured, it can't be improved" is applicable even in the context of parish ministry. Therefore, it's incumbent on the congregation and its vestry to identify prospectively the benchmarks that will enable it to document success and failures and adjust its missional strategy accordingly.

Finally, and perhaps most frequently overlooked in the development of mission statements, are brevity and the need to be memorable. Those that function best in the life of a congregation (or any organization) are succinct, capturing the parish's ministry in as few words as possible, in language that is hopeful and grounded in the Gospel, and in a way that is readily recalled by the entire congregation.

The vestry's role is pivotal in the development of a parish mission statement. It's the sieve through which the congregation's hopes are filtered. It's the artisan that molds them into a cohesive statement of ministerial purpose. And it's the guide that frames the collective response to St. Teresa's challenge to be Jesus' eyes, hands, and feet in a world that longs for justice, mercy, and peace.

Vestry Discussion

- Does Teresa of Ávila's perspective shape your understanding of the mission of the Church and our responsibility to enact it? If so, how?
- What might the vestry do to focus, facilitate, and energize your mission and ministries?
- How should progress in achieving your mission be measured and documented?

Something to Ponder

A congregation's mission ultimately falls short if its lay and clergy leaders fail to engage it in tangible and visible ways, modeling for the parish and larger community the aspirations they hold for the future. You're invited to reflect on the phrase "walk the talk" as you consider your congregation's vision and how best to pursue it.

Values Drive Decisions

Opening Prayer

Almighty God, who has called us to lead the faithful of our parish, equip us to embrace even the most difficult of challenges we confront with grace, love, and wisdom; the values that undergird our vision and mission; and a collegial spirit in resolving the issues that come before us. For the sake of all whom we serve, we pray in Jesus' Name. Amen.

A Quote for Your Consideration

Congregational decision-making reflects all the challenges of a complex organization. Although some of the questions are straightforward and readily answered, many are nuanced, multifaceted, and often contentious. Clearly, a parish's vision for the future, as well as its explicit statement of mission—its distinct role in realizing that future—provide the foundation for church policy and administrative discussions. However, seldom are they alone capable of offering the specificity required for analyzing complicated issues or resolving the competing priorities they embody.

For example, a vision to "ensure justice for all" doesn't necessarily include sponsoring a legal services clinic. Consequently, a more robust and complementary framework that incorporates a congregation's consistent priorities—its values—is essential. Considering the previous illustration, a congregation that holds public education and legislative advocacy on issues of social justice as a core value would likely reach a different conclusion than one that places a priority on offering *pro bono* legal services to marginalized persons. Eighteenth-century "man of letters" and author of the first English-language dictionary Samuel Johnson understood the importance of decisions consistently grounded in the tenets to which we ascribe (2002):

> It is not difficult to conceive, however, that for many reasons a man writes much better than he lives. For, without entering into refined speculations, it may be shown much easier to design than perform. A man proposes his schemes of life in a state of abstraction

and disengagement, exempt from the enticements of hope, the solicitations of affection, the importunities of appetite, or the depressions of fear, and is in the same state with him that teaches upon land the art of navigation, to whom the sea is always smooth, and the wind always prosperous ... We are, therefore, not to wonder that most fail, amidst tumult and snares and danger, in the observance of those precepts, which they laid down in solitude, safety, and tranquility, with a mind unbiased, and with liberty unobstructed ... Nothing is more unjust, however uncommon, than to charge with hypocrisy him that expresses zeal for those virtues which he neglects to practice; since he may be sincerely convinced of the advantages of conquering his passions, without having yet obtained the victory.

Leadership in Context

In the context of organizational planning and leadership, values are understood to be those several distinct principles that are central to the way the institution functions and its decision-making processes. Faith communities share this ethos. The challenge for congregations is how to define those values to which they're fundamentally committed (i.e., given precedence over others) as they engage routine, as well as difficult, questions of church policy.

To be sure, Scripture is replete with examples of the values faith communities should embrace—love, mercy, justice, and hospitality, to name only a few. However, simply appropriating them as the guideposts for decision-making is fraught with problems. On the one hand, it could rightfully be argued that each of these is to be understood as God's unqualified gift and applied without condition in the ministries of the Church. Yet on the other, while acknowledging God's unlimited abundance, no single individual or faith community can marshal all of it. Rather, individual churches are called to allocate the full abundance of the *specific* gifts and resources God has shared with them consistent with their vision and mission. And this requires values that are precise, actionable, and reflective of both the reality and imagination of the congregation. Indeed, values define the range of choices (but frequently not the sole choice) available as vestries respond to particular issues.

I'm reminded of a congregation that promotes itself as, "welcoming and inclusive of all." For almost a year, a young, unhoused man regularly attended worship services and gradually began to participate quietly in the parish's fellowship and formation programs. Eventually, he sought to be confirmed and was. With winter approaching, the question arose among the clergy and vestry of how they might demonstrate their hospitality and inclusivity with this newest member of the community. Clergy proposed providing him with safe space on the church's campus for his sleeping bag and few personal belongings, with daily access to the bathroom and, on especially cold nights, to a heated conference room. Although a written agreement was signed, it soon became apparent that the individual was not complying with its terms and was increasingly perceived by some staff and congregants as threatening. A contentious debate ensued among the clergy and vestry—one finally resolved by rescinding the agreement and the young man's decision to move to a warmer climate.

In retrospect, the decision-making process was fraught with pitfalls, not the least of which was that the congregation's mission of universal welcome had not been refined to provide more direct guidance in its application. Developing a congregational statement of values is not easy. The possibilities are virtually limitless, as is the language that gives it meaning. The process begins with a conversation grounded in the parish's vision and mission, exploring potential principles that could facilitate their implementation. They're massaged to capture the breadth and depth of the congregation's commitment to them and to focus attention on those few that truly are at the faith community's spiritual core. They're word-smithed for inspiration, brevity, and ease of practical application. They're tested and validated in the context of the vestry's actual decision-making process. And finally, they're widely communicated to the congregation and larger community, as well as explicitly referenced in the explanation of the vestry's significant policy and governance decisions. While a daunting task, Elihu's exhortation to Job (34.4) provides the necessary encouragement for this critical work: "Let us choose what is right; let us determine among ourselves what is good."

Vestry Discussion

- What values are central to your personal, family, and professional life? Do any take consistent precedence? If so, which one(s) and why?
- What congregational values take priority in your leadership? Why?

- Does the congregation know its values, and if not, how might this be addressed?
- How might the vestry communicate its decisions in the context of the congregation's values?

Something to Ponder

At its best, vestry decision-making reflects not only a consistent process for addressing policy and administrative issues but also the core principles that ground the congregation's life together. However, values often compete against each other in specific circumstances. Consequently, you're invited to consider "competing values" and how they can be reconciled in complex vestry deliberations.

Beyond Fiduciary Responsibilities

Opening Prayer

Guide us, O thou great Jehovah. Instill in us love, generosity, and the deepest care for the Church, the parish we serve, and those whose lives we touch. Grant us wisdom, the breadth of imagination, and an openness to the Truth you share. And focus our uncompromised loyalty and commitment to you, the Church throughout the world, and our congregation. All for Jesus' sake. Amen.

A Quote for Your Consideration

The governance of a faith community is complicated, drawing on its ecclesiastical tradition, local history, and legal structure. Except for those relatively few that abhor any internal or external oversight, virtually all accept some authoritative process that ensures the integrity of faith and worship, as well as accountability for the human and capital resources that enable its mission. The nature of this authority and the way in which it's exercised in no small measure define our perception of the Church—the Body of Christ—and our stewardship of the infinite gifts bestowed on us by a bountiful God. How we understand and use this authority is succinctly captured by the twentieth-century Anglican priest Charles Gore (2002), renowned mediator of Church tradition and modernism:

> True authority does not issue edict to suppress men's personal judgment or render its actions unnecessary, but it is like the authority of a parent, which invigorates and encourages, even while it restrains and guides the growth of our own individuality.

Leadership in Context

Jesus' ministry prior to his Passion is largely characterized by prophetic witness, teaching, and healing. It often occurs in the context of personal or small-group interaction but also addresses the corruption of institutions and those who lead them, most notably in his "cleansing of the Temple":

> The Passover of the Jews was near, and Jesus went up to Jerusalem. In the temple he found people selling

cattle, sheep, and doves, and the money changers seated at their tables. Making a whip of cords, he drove all of them out of the temple, both the sheep and the cattle. He also poured out the coins of the money changers and overturned their tables. He told those who were selling the doves, "Take these things out of here! Stop making my Father's house a marketplace!" His disciples remembered that it was written, "Zeal for your house will consume me" (John 2.13–17).

Jesus was outraged not only by the violation of the Temple's sanctity but also by the leadership that condoned it. The model of Temple governance originally imposed by God on the people of Israel clearly had collapsed, and strong action was warranted. Consequently, this example alone should summon us to explore more fully the responsibilities vestries hold for governing the life of the congregations they serve.

In the context of organizational governance, vestries are odd ducks. They don't have shareholders whose relative financial investment determines the extent of their influence over corporate policy and management (at least officially). Nor do they hold the legal charter that enables for-profit corporate activity. And although they share the breadth of fiduciary duties that ground the work of corporate boards, vestries also have responsibility for the spiritual formation of their parishes. Even among other not-for-profit entities, they differ. The shared leadership of the vestry and rector, for example, the ready access of staff to individual members of the vestry and the extent of oversight by a regional diocese and the national church distinguish them from many other organizations.

Although vestries are not corporate boards of directors, they nonetheless have legal and ecclesiastical responsibilities in governing their congregations. Despite the differences in organizational structure and obligations, however, the governance reforms initiated by the 2002 Sarbanes-Oxley Act passed by Congress in the wake of several accounting scandals—Enron, Tyco International, WorldCom, and others—provide guidance that also is useful in the complex system of vestry leadership.

Whether intentionally or not, vestries can be perceived by the parishioners they serve as isolated if not secretive, hoarding information to which they feel entitled and not fully justifying the decisions they make. The philosopher Ralph Waldo Emerson and Supreme Court Justice Louis D. Brandeis are jointly credited with coining the phrase, "Sunshine is the best disinfectant." Arguably, full transparency truly is essential to the decision-making processes of vestries and the integrity of their leadership. The information and data provided to them must be as complete as reasonably possible, with any material omissions fully noted and explained. Likewise, their decisions must be clearly justified and should routinely be communicated to the congregation—with the notable exception of personnel issues. In addition, a mechanism for feedback and response to questions raised by parishioners should be an integral component of the governance process.

Differentiating between a governing body's recognized role in organizational strategy and policy and management's responsibility for their execution is especially challenging for vestries. While financial oversight is common to virtually all governance structures, vestries frequently find themselves in the weeds of parish operations—worship, building and grounds, and outreach, for example—often necessitated by a staff too small to support all that needs to be accomplished or the complexity of the tasks themselves. Unavoidable though vestry engagement in operational planning may be, it's imperative that members understand their role as advisory, assuming specific responsibilities only in collaboration with the rector.

In the corporate world, it was historically suggested that the sole responsibilities of the board of directors were to hire the CEO and ensure the integrity of the financial statements. Certainly, in the two decades since the enactment of Sarbanes-Oxley, the requirements of governance have expanded significantly. Nevertheless, the regular evaluation of the senior executive officer of the corporation remains critical. And it's no different for churches. How it's accomplished, however, is a particular challenge. An individual evaluation of the rector by the senior warden, with the results reported to the entire vestry, is perhaps the most common. A review by a committee of the vestry that is then shared with all its members also is frequently employed.

Unfortunately, several crucial elements are frequently absent in the performance evaluation of rectors that potentially undermine its credibility. First, are the specific metrics (performance measures) for the evaluation mutually agreed upon by the rector and vestry? Absent these pre-determined standards, the rector's review can easily be shaped by individual bias and subjective assessment. Second, as both investor-controlled and not-for-profit organizations have increasingly incorporated 360-degree reviews in performance appraisals for senior leaders, vestries would be well-advised to design and implement a constructive process for staff and members of the congregation to contribute to the rector's review.

Although vestry members bring a wealth of personal and professional experience to their ministry, the social, ecclesiastical, and legal environment in which they work is constantly shifting. Therefore, ensuring the continuing education of vestries—including orientation to the vestry's roles and responsibilities, the leadership development of its members, governance competence, and spiritual growth—should be a priority. The resources available inexpensively online and through YouTube and other hardcopy and electronic platforms offer incredible possibilities for enriching the vestry's understanding of and approach to its unique ministry. As a component of their ongoing education, vestries also should consider a standardized, regular self-assessment of their work and discussion of the opportunities for improvement.

Clearly, these four elements of progressive, "best practices" governance—transparency, role differentiation, performance evaluation, and continuing education—are only several of the critical components of responsible lay leadership in faith communities. And although rooted in the corporate world, they provide an essential foundation for the integrity and credibility of a vestry's work, as well as the trust and confidence of the parish in response to its decisions.

Vestry Discussion

- How do worship, prayers, and study shape your leadership of the congregation and your vestry ministry?
- Conversely, how has your service on the vestry shaped your spiritual life?
- Is the work of your vestry regularly and broadly communicated throughout your congregation? If not, why not?
- What facets of your vestry's governance could be improved? How?

Something to Ponder

Learning to govern effectively is both an individual and organizational challenge. We each bring distinct perspectives and unique experiences to this ministry. Likewise, the congregation has its own institutional memory and "way of doing things." How to integrate these diverse views into a model of governance that enables the vestry to till new ground and respond to new issues while maintaining continuity with the congregation's past is a question that each vestry cohort will need to address. Therefore, you're invited to consider "duty" as you reflect on the vestry's work.

. . . And God Laughs

Opening Prayer

O God, whose hopes for us exceed all we deserve and can even imagine: grant us the capacity to learn from the past; give us clear vision and a humble spirit as we assess the present; and open us to new possibilities for the future and our ability to shape it. All this we ask in the Name of Christ, our Lord. Amen.

A Quote for Your Consideration

Among the most important tasks of parish governance is strategic planning, a systematic process that enables an organization to (1) develop goals and actionable objectives for a finite period consistent with its vision, mission, and values; (2) articulate the means to achieve them; and (3) establish the measures of success. Although at first glance this might appear to be corporate intrusion into the spiritual domain of the Church, the wisdom of the late Yankees baseball catcher and homeplate philosopher Yogi Berra counsels otherwise: "If you don't know where you are going, you might wind up someplace else."

Having a clear sense of direction, marshaling the resources necessary to move forward, and mobilizing support are as important to Apple, the Mayo Clinic, and the Gates Foundation as they are to the congregations we serve. And it begins with strategic leadership from the corporate C-suite and, in our parishes, from clergy and vestries. The framework and tools for strategic planning have emerged from the business community over the past century and been studied by scholars from a variety of disciplines. While several models exist for structuring the planning process and focusing its outcomes, the generic core common to each provides an appropriate context for a discussion of their application to the work and ministry of the Church.

Leadership in Context

For thirty-five years before I was ordained a priest, I was privileged with a wonderful career in health-care academic and executive leadership in positions frequently responsible for organizational strategic planning. I relished the challenge of trying to understand what our patients, caregivers, and employees needed, what the community, businesses, and insurers wanted, and what we could provide. It truly was a continual game of 3D chess, with the sobering reminder that our work had profound implications for the lives of every person our organizations touched. And when done thoughtfully, communicated effectively, and broadly embraced, these strategic plans rightfully guided the myriad critical decisions we made, as well as provided the template for necessary mid-course corrections. So important is this cornerstone of leadership that the late Charles Knight, chairman and CEO of Emerson Electric, one of the nation's most successful companies, often described his management style by simply stating that "I'll look over your plan. I'll look over your budget. But I won't look over your shoulder." While learning from our corporate colleagues, how then might clergy and vestry customize the generic elements of strategic planning for use in their congregations?

Strategic planning and arguably all organizational life begin with an aspirational vision, an explicit mission, and the specific values that will guide decision-making and facilitate the resolution of competing priorities. Too often these organizational statements are mere platitudes posted on our websites, casually referenced in stewardship campaigns and otherwise generally ignored in the routine work of being church. Although these may be the most elusive ingredients in the strategic planning mix, it's imperative that congregational leaders strive for precision, since ultimately it's vision, mission, and values that will be the foundation for success and the backdrop against which that success is measured.

Understanding the reality of the community and larger cultural environment in which a parish is or expects to be functioning is essential to providing a realistic context for the development of a strategic plan. What forces locally enhance or impede your congregation's capacity for ministry and outreach—worship style, preaching, community engagement, education, social justice advocacy, location, and parking, to name only a few? More broadly, what trends in organizational participation (including in the life of the Church) might impact the future of your congregation? To what extent does the purported distinction between being "spiritual but not religious" provide or limit opportunities for evangelism that truly unlocks the Good News of Jesus Christ? And can the many attractions that compete for the public's time and attention be effectively challenged by a creative and robust congregational presence?

Equally as important to the strategic planning process is a comprehensive and accurate assessment of the congregation's current position and ministries, the resources available to support its reach, and reasonable prospects for the future. This analysis of organizational strengths, weaknesses, opportunities, and threats (SWOT) should be driven by both quantitative data wherever available and qualitative information gained through the experience and perceptions of the clergy, vestry, congregation, and community. Perhaps the biggest challenge in this phase of the planning process is the rejoinder to "always question your own publicity!" Despite our rightful pride in what our congregations have accomplished, there's always ample room for innovation and improvement.

Translating environmental scanning and a SWOT analysis into a cohesive and comprehensive strategic plan should readily flow from the data, information, and discussions that evolved earlier in the process. To ensure that the plan is consistent with and advances the congregation's vision, mission, and values, the planning document should begin with a "high-level" overview of how this will be accomplished, followed by four integrated components. Goals reflect the future state of the organization if the plan is successfully accomplished—for example, "to be a congregation fully immersed in the study of Scripture and reflection on it." To achieve the goals, actionable objectives and schedules are established that, in the previous illustration, might include "for 10% of the congregation to complete *The Bible Challenge: Read the Bible in a Year* by December 31, 2026." Action steps guide the organization to conduct what is necessary to accomplish the objectives; for example, "register at least 10% of the congregation for *The Bible Challenge: Read the Bible in a Year* by November 30, 2025." The final component of this planning grid should include a specific measure of success; for example "10% of the congregation completed *The Bible Challenge: Read the Bible in a Year* by December 31, 2026."

Several cautions are noteworthy. First, I long ago learned the value of the "economy of goals and objectives"; that is, ensuring that they are highly focused, few, and, although a "stretch," achievable. Nothing is more organizationally disabling than a plan that's overwhelming and unattainable. Additionally, the ideal planning horizon is three to five years, beyond which it's difficult to anticipate the nature and pace of change, and speculation too readily replaces informed analysis. Likewise, the time frames established in the plan need to be realistic even as they summon aggressive implementation. And although the elements of spiritual growth and renewal essential to the future of a faith community are far too often ignored in a strategic plan largely focused on administrative functions, they are critical to the congregational life we share.

Also frequently overlooked or given short shrift are the physical preparation and presentation of the strategic plan and its communication to the entire congregation and, when appropriate, external stakeholders. The time and resources invested in the layout and graphic design of the plan, as well as a comprehensive approach for disseminating, reviewing, and modifying it, are vital to its integrity and embrace by the parish and larger community it serves.

Finally, I'm reminded of the Yiddish proverb: "We make plans and God laughs!" Consider Jeremiah's plan to do something other than be God's prophet, or Paul's (nee Saul's) intent to persecute Christians in Damascus. We are wise to accept that the unpredictable of the world around us, not to mention

Divine intervention, regularly intrudes into our carefully conceived plans. And consequently, we're obligated in our strategic planning process to account for the occasional need to change direction and revise priorities, a lesson proffered in the first chapters of the Hebrew Scriptures. We can debate, for example, whether the creation narrative is the result of God's forethought and planning or evolved incrementally as God introduced each feature. What seems to be clear, however, is that God stepped back and reassessed the result of the work that had been done, eventually concluding, "It is not good that the man should be alone; I will make him a helper as his partner" (Genesis 2.18). Thanks be to God for the course correction!

Unlike organizational operations, which are generally discreet and linear, strategic planning is a highly integrated process involving cobbling together often disparate inputs into a map for the future with the recognition that detours are inevitable. President Dwight Eisenhower declared that "plans are worthless, but planning is everything." Perhaps tongue-in-cheek or hyperbole, his counsel nevertheless punctuates the critical importance of engaging in it for the sake of our congregations and the world in which we're called to serve.

Vestry Discussion

- When has "God laughed" at your plans or those of your parish? How did you respond?
- How does your vestry maintain an openness to the Spirit moving among it as it wills even as you're

attempting to define and structure the congregation's future?
- Does your congregation have a strategic plan? If so, how does your vestry engage the parish and community in the strategic planning process?
- Do you regularly use the strategic plan as a guide in vestry decision-making? If not, why?

Something to Ponder

Done well, strategic plans are meant to be living documents—frequently consulted, regularly used, and routinely revised to reflect changing circumstances. Toward that end, you're invited to consider "nimbleness" as a critical aspect of strategic planning and the life of your congregation.

AROUND THE CHURCH

The Servant Who Leads or the Leader Who Serves?

Opening Prayer

God of infinite understanding, wisdom, and courage: guide our deliberations that they may ever be grounded in the Gospel; embrace the needs of our congregation, community, and world; and empower ministries of faith, justice, and peace. All for the love of our Lord, Jesus Christ. Amen.

A Quote for Your Consideration

Leadership is central to the work of a vestry and its individual members acting in concert. The parish expects it of us and, hopefully, we do of ourselves and each other. Importantly, it also is the Father's expectation of us, as well as Jesus'. In reflecting on your own leadership style, the principles that guide it, and the opportunities for both personal and congregational growth, you're invited to consider the following quote from Roman Catholic priest, theologian, and advocate for the disabled Henri Nouwen (1977). "If we accept leadership it can only be honest if it takes the form of service."

Leadership in Context

Although the concept of "servant leadership" has gained prominence in the academic and popular literature in recent decades, it's deeply rooted in the Biblical canon. Perhaps most revealing is Mark's Gospel (10.42–45), in which Jesus gives clear voice to it:

> So Jesus called them and said to them, "You know that among the Gentiles those whom they recognize as their rulers lord it over them, and their great ones are tyrants over them. But it is not so among you; but whoever wishes to become great among you must be your servant, and whoever wishes to be first among you must be slave of all. For the Son of Man came not to be served but to serve, and to give his life a ransom for many."

In declaring his own servanthood and simultaneously exhorting his followers to adopt the same posture if they're to lead, Jesus transformed not only the meaning of service but also the social contract in which it had developed in the ancient world. In the Torah and other early books of the Hebrew Scriptures, we're informed that service is an activity that occurs in a hierarchy, performed by individuals of lower status to aid those who hold authority over them (Pilch 2003). Regardless of their status as a slave or free person, compensated or not, service is the work of those perceived to be socially inferior in support of the social, economic, religious, and political elite.

It would be a mistake, however, to limit the Biblical concept of servanthood to secular relationships. Notable, for example, are those who were designated by God as servants of the Divine—Abraham, Moses, and David among them. While preserving the hierarchy in which the servant is subordinate, the work is to glorify God and the pursuit of harmony among all creation and, as such, elevate the status of the servant. The introduction of the servant's suffering for God's sake in Isaiah adds yet another dimension to this evolving concept and presages Jesus' ministry. Finally, the life of the early church recorded in the New Testament's Acts of the Apostles and the subsequent epistles clarifies servanthood in the context of the emerging community of faith, begins to institutionalize it in the appointment of deacons and ministers, and reminds us of the dangers of serving for the sake of the Gospel.

With the relationship between service and leadership clearly established across the arc of Scripture, it's not surprising that contemporary organizational and managerial theorists have attempted to develop a consensus definition of *servant leadership*, determine its fundamental characteristics, and test its validity in multiple settings. Although tangentially referenced in religious, political, and economic discourses for centuries, the concept was brought to the attention of a broader audience in Robert Greenleaf's 1983 book, *Servant Leadership: A Journey into the Nature of Legitimate Power and Greatness*. In it, he asserted the primacy of service, with the capacity to lead dependent on the leader's understanding of the needs of others, willingness to subordinate personal desires, and the embrace of the leader by those who follow.

Indeed, the most effective leaders are those who understand their vocation as a call to service, with leadership the means of executing this call.

However, the question of what constitutes servanthood remains. What are its components, determinants, and their interrelationships? And how can we best study the impact of this servant leadership in organizations in which it's practiced? The past 25 years have witnessed significant growth in research on these critical questions, with many proposing specific formulations. Among the most persuasive is the argument proffered by Eva and colleagues (2019) asserting that servant leadership should be consistently defined as "an (1) other-oriented approach to leadership (2) manifested through one-on-one prioritizing of follower individual needs and interests, (3) and outward reorienting of their concern for self toward concern for others within the organization and larger community." The authors also proposed three dimensions to servant leadership, specifically the leader's motivation for assuming that role; how the needs of others are prioritized; and the mindset of the leader, focusing on the ability to empower others in the foundational commitment to service.

Although various scales have been developed to measure servant leadership within both not-for-profit and commercial enterprises, it remains for many something that needs to be experienced to be understood. I'm reminded of the newly minted CEO of a health-care organization who early in his tenure realized the substantial travel credits and benefits accrued by the senior staff in their work were retained by them for their personal use. Meeting with them, he developed unanimous agreement that those rewards were earned in the service of the organization and, therefore, should be distributed across the workforce. Shortly thereafter, he announced to the entire staff that the credits gained from senior staff travel would be pooled and given away in an annual drawing. Everyone would be eligible ... except the CEO and senior staff. At his retirement years later, staff still remarked on this single gesture and its impact on employee trust and morale.

Clearly, servant leadership can be practiced in any organization. However, several characteristics especially commend it to life in the Church. Perhaps most important, it reflects Jesus' approach to his own ministry. The exhortation to his disciples (Mark 10.42–45) noted earlier and Jesus' washing of the disciples' feet at his final meal with them (John 13.12–14) poignantly illustrate his humility and selflessness. If our journey of faith is to become increasingly more like Jesus (and I believe it is), then adopting his leadership style is an essential component of our growth and evolving spiritual maturity. In addition, while parish life is grounded in worship and prayer, it also embodies the care of each other and service to those beyond our walls. Understanding their needs and subrogating our own individual and collective desires is the pastoral exercise of servant leadership. Finally, it's incumbent on clergy and congregational leaders to cultivate the next generation—a challenge for which the servant leadership model is ideally suited.

Certainly, leaders develop their own styles based on their personality, values, and experiences. However, organizations—through their cultures and priorities—also can set explicit expectations for leaders, as well as those who follow. Toward that end, vestries are encouraged to develop a leadership charter for themselves, the clergy, and staff specifying the general shape and context of leadership in the parish and the behaviors necessary to function successfully. Second, it's imperative that opportunities to learn servant leadership and apply it be supported by the congregation. And last, incorporating the dimensions of servant leadership into regular self-evaluations and organizational performance appraisals will facilitate a culture of servanthood by holding ourselves and each other accountable for it.

Vestry Discussion

- What is your leadership style, and is it consistent across the various communities to which you belong (e.g., family, work, church, etc.)? What values ground it?
- Does Jesus' ministry inform your leadership? If so, how? What elements of his ministry do you find problematic, if any?
- In your role as a member of the vestry, do you see yourself *primarily* as a servant? Why or why not?
- Should servant leadership be the expectation of your parish? If so, how might it be cultivated?

Something to Ponder

At the core of servant leadership is placing the needs of others above ours—emptying ourselves so that we can make room to understand and respond to the concerns of the world we inhabit. As you reflect on your leadership of the parish, you're invited to consider how "self-emptying" might shape your faith and ministry.

What Makes Space Sacred?

Opening Prayer

God of stalwart presence whose Son Jesus Christ "is made the sure foundation" of the Church, grant us foresight and wisdom to discern how best our facilities might be used to further the ministry to which we have been called in this time and this place. Open our eyes to new possibilities for our building and grounds even as we faithfully maintain their integrity for all who find solace and comfort in its walls and on its paths. "To this temple, where we call thee, come, O Lord of Hosts, today; with thy wonted loving kindness hear thy servants as they pray, and thy fullest benediction shed within its walls alway" (*The Hymnal 1982*, #518, "Christ is made the sure foundation"). Amen.

A Quote for Your Consideration

Among the most challenging aspects of congregational governance is the stewardship of its physical facilities—the building and grounds. Regardless of their age, size, or design, each has issues that call for constant attention. Older structures too often suffer from long-deferred maintenance, outdated and inefficient mechanical systems, and a street address far from the current location of its members. Others were constructed during the nominal "Golden Age" of church attendance in the 1950s and, perhaps except for Christmas and Easter, have more vacant than filled pews on Sunday mornings. Many were designed for dated and relatively rigid liturgical expressions rather than the more flexible approaches of the past few decades. Especially disconcerting, however, is the number of churches that are burdened by several or all of these.

To be sure, church buildings have many functions—worship, formation, administration, and community engagement among them. At their core, however, is the provision of space for the individual and communal worship of God—sacred space for the encounter of the Divine. The other functions, while essential to the life of the parish and its ministries, are secondary. So, in considering how best to care for and use these buildings, it's critical that we first understand what makes space sacred. Anglican liturgical scholar Susan J. White offers an especially thoughtful and intriguing invitation into this conversation. "Worship the Lord in the beauty of holiness" has most often been turned into "worship the Lord in the holiness of beauty" (2002).

Leadership in Context

'Wanna start a real congregational kerfuffle? Then propose relocating the altar, switching out pews for chairs, or removing the communion rail. For the most part, we love our church buildings . . . often to a fault. They can be places of remarkable beauty and grandeur. They can be humble structures with well-worn cushions and tattered paraments. Or they can be nondescript boxes with little to distinguish them architecturally.

Regardless of their physical appearance, however, these buildings are cherished for the memories they hold, the experiences they embrace, and the faith formed within their walls. Truly, we understand them to be sacred, holy spaces. Coupled with our generally reflexive resistance to change, it's easy to understand that tampering with them—even slightly, even necessarily—needs to be approached with caution. And it's not just those highly visible changes that merit careful attention. It's also the more nuanced ones—updating HVAC systems that require relocating walls, installing electronic technology that disrupts ceilings and floors, and insulating exterior doors and windows, for example.

As White observed, our ability to respond to the physical needs of our buildings and grounds is often hampered by imbuing "sacredness" to bricks, mortar, and land themselves. But is this "holiness" an intrinsic characteristic of the elements of construction, a quality endowed through ecclesiastical consecration, a function of the actions that occur within these structures, or some intricate interaction among them?

In his 2004 analysis of the historical development of liturgical architecture, Richard Giles emphasized the actions of the faithful Christian community within the confines of the church as fundamental to the presence of that which is sacred, evidenced in seven specific movements. Foundational is the recognition that sacred space is defined by the community gathering for common purpose, witness, and mission. In addition, it is a liturgical assembly into which individuals are initiated and where the Word is proclaimed and bread is broken. Sacred space also is characterized by the presence of an individual authorized to preside over the Eucharist. It is a place for prayer and music that mine the depth and breadth of the human condition, as well as the majesty, mercy, and mystery of the Triune God. Finally, in and through these movements, space is sanctified by its capacity to form the gathered community for ministry to one another, as well as to the larger society in which it is an integral component.

The Biblical witness consistently supports this understanding of sacred space defined by what's done in it, with the construction of altars made sacred by the sacrifices offered on them a frequent example. The Psalmist (84.3) exquisitely captures this relationship:

> Even the sparrow finds a home
> > and the swallow a nest for herself,
> > where she may lay her young,
> at your altars, O Lord of hosts,
> > my King and my God.

Alternatively, Jesus made abundantly clear that certain actions can defile otherwise holy ground.

> Then Jesus entered the temple and drove out all who were selling and buying in the temple, and he overturned the tables of the money changers and the seats of those who sold doves. He said to them, "It is written, 'My house shall be called a house of prayer'; but you are making it a den of robbers" (Matthew 21.12–13).

Although a broad consensus of liturgical scholars supports the sacredness of space as defined by the actions that occur within it, attention also has focused on the source of the work that enables this movement: God, the gathered community, or a combination of both. In its rite for "The Dedication and Consecration of a Church," The Book of Common Prayer (1979) speaks directly to the distinctiveness of church space, emphasized in the prayer immediately following the bishop's opening exhortation: ". . . Receive the work of our hands in this place, now to be set apart for your worship . . ." The rite clearly intends that the church and its furnishings are to be dedicated specifically to the veneration and celebration of God—in baptism, the proclamation of the Word, and the celebration of the Eucharist. In fact, the prayer of the congregational representative punctuates just this point: "Lord Jesus Christ, make this a temple of *your presence* (emphasis added) and a house of prayer." However, this same prayer continues, "Be always near us when *we seek* (emphasis added) you in this place," punctuating the collective liturgical action characteristic of the Church. Thus, while the church and its appointments have been "set apart" for worship with the expectation that God will be encountered, it's equally apparent that this Presence is realized through the actions of the faithful, ". . . alone or when we come with others . . . ."

The implication for vestries in their consideration of issues related to the stewardship of a congregation's building and grounds is clear. The bricks, mortar, and land are to be held in trust as a physical manifestation of the work of God and the faithful there. And, they are made sacred by that work, not by any intrinsic quality or inherent beauty. Therefore, whether assessing significant changes or those that seem inconsequential, the fundamental question to be resolved is what most enhances God's work and the people's.

Vestry Discussion

- How do you understand "church" in your life, faith, and vestry leadership?
- What impact do church buildings and grounds where you worship have on your spirituality? How?
- Do your building and grounds offer new possibilities for ministry or limit your vision?

Something to Ponder

The stewardship of sacred space is a complex challenge for vestries. As you consider the many issues embedded in the care of building and grounds, you're invited to reflect on "bricks and mortar" as a vital component of your leadership of the parish.

The Work of the People

Opening Prayer

God of majesty whose glory commands our worship and praise: grace us with your indefatigable love; fill us with the richness and depth of your Spirit; show us the holiness of all you have created; and move us to celebrate you with every fiber of our being. In Jesus' Name we humbly pray. Amen.

A Quote for Your Consideration

Although the authority of clergy extends to communal worship and the music it embodies, wise priests—and certainly those aspiring to a lengthy tenure—know that consultation with the congregation's leadership is essential to ensuring that both reflect the sensibilities of the parish, as well as denominational requirements. So, too, does such collaboration provide the opportunity to explore potential liturgical changes in a supportive context. Any cleric who's ever introduced new musical instruments, hymns, or liturgies without prepping the congregational soil knows the extent to which familiarity and tradition are closely held and not readily challenged. In fact, I'm reminded of a Lutheran pastor who wanted to make the principal Sunday service "more relevant" and introduced a praise band and large video screens in the sanctuary for the congregation to follow the liturgy and hymns. Although he had the approval of his Board of Elders, the congregation was caught off guard. Not surprisingly, the complaints resounded throughout this faith community, and several families left, declaring, "If I wanted a Baptist service, I'd go to a Baptist church!" So, it's within this context that nineteenth-century Anglican theologian and founder of the Christian Socialist movement Frederick Denison Maurice offers especially wise counsel to clergy and lay leaders alike (2002b):

> I hope you will never hear from me such phrases as "our incomparable liturgy": I do not think we are to praise the liturgy but to use it. When we do not want it for our life, we may begin to talk of it as a beautiful

composition. Thanks be to God, it does not remind us of its own merits when it is bidding us draw near to him.

Leadership in Context

Let's face it. We've gotten sloppy with our language around church and worship ... and not to our benefit. We "go to church," for example, reflecting both a physical presence and the worship that occurs within its walls. So, too, do we regularly use "worship" to denote the liturgical actions in a ritual service, often ignoring its much broader and less structured application to the celebration of all that God is and has created. Add words like *services* and *liturgy* to the mix and we have a bit of a muddled mess that's confusing and, if not clarified, imperils the ability of a congregation and its leaders to understand their work in worship and explore opportunities to enrich it.

From the earliest days of ancient Israel, the faithful have been summoned to worship. The Chronicler bids us to "ascribe to the Lord the glory due his name; bring an offering, and come before him. Worship the Lord in holy splendor..." (1 Chronicles 16.29). Similarly, the Psalmist invites us, "O come, let us worship and bow down, let us kneel before the Lord, our Maker!" (Psalm 95.6). Although the explicit rubrics for worship in these passages are limited to almsgiving, bowing, and kneeling, they nonetheless reveal the central feature of worship: action by the people in response to the unbridled love, mercy, and grace previously initiated by

God, a precept eloquently expressed by the Roman Catholic liturgical scholar Aidan Kavanagh (1984).

> Therefore Christians do not worship because they believe. They believe because the One in whose gift faith lies is regularly met in the act of communal worship—not because the assembly conjures up God, but because the initiative lies with the God who has promised to be there always. The *lex credendi* [law of belief] is thus subordinated to the *lex supplicandi* [law of supplication] because both standards exist and function only within the worshipping assembly's own subordination of itself to its ever-present Judge, Savior, and unifying Spirit.

Clearly, God is the focus of our worship, but the question of context remains. Recognizing the breadth of settings and activities encompassed by the concept of worship, what are its distinguishing characteristics? What, for example, is common to an individual's humble reflection on the majesty of the towering mountains and rushing streams God has created and the shared celebration of the Eucharist in a small, out-of-the-way village? Arguably, it's an encounter with the holy. It's the experience of being completely enveloped by the unqualified and unique presence of God as Creator, Redeemer, and Sanctifier. And it's our full-throated embrace of the eternally saving grace freely gifted by God. The awe of a baby robin emerging from the nest for the first time, the depth of gratitude on the face of a troubled teen saved by the quick action of a paramedic and the administration of Narcan, and the personal joy of listening to music that lifts the soul and transports us into communion with God—each occasion inspires the wonder of worship.

Amid the variety of encounters with the holy, the Rev. Dr. Donald Gray, Canon Emeritus of Westminster Abbey and former chaplain to the British Speaker of the House of Commons, has posited six characteristics that either individually or in combination describe the broad experience of worship (2000): adoration; confession of sin; proclamation and thanksgiving; confession of faith; intercession; and expectation. The unlimited ways in which these can be engaged further amplifies the ubiquitous nature of worship.

However, as important as it is to acknowledge the infinite opportunities for worship in the individual encounter with the holy, worship is most fully experienced in community as we listen, learn, sing, and pray together. Not surprisingly, as Israel's tradition of Temple worship evolved, it became more ritualized and consistent. With the translation of the Hebrew Scriptures into the Greek Septuagint several centuries before the birth of Christ, *leitourgia* (liturgy), "the work of the people," emerged as the description of this communal worship, language subsequently adopted by New Testament authors.

The late Episcopal liturgical scholars Charles P. Price and Louis Weil (2000) pointedly observed that:

> Christ's life of obedience and death on the cross is the Christian liturgy, replacing the liturgy of the temple. His life and death are the ultimate work for the people, their redemption from sin and death, at

the ultimate private cost, the complete obedience to the point of death of the one whom we acknowledge to be the Son of God.

While these distinguished authors offer a profound truth, our contemporary use of liturgy has evolved into a description of the prescribed actions that make up a communal worship service. Echoing Maurice's earlier point, Price and Weil focus on how liturgy is used, on the actions that shape it and give it meaning in the context of the Christian faith. Like Jesus', our lives are to be grounded in sacrifice, celebrating His gift once and forever in the Eucharist and daily lived in and shared with the world. Although individuals ordained to the priesthood lead liturgical worship, the "work of the people" truly is accomplished by the priesthood of all believers. Prayer also features in the liturgy, regardless of its form, and reflects our unambiguous conviction of the perfection of Christ's sacrifice. Finally, Price and Weil remind us of the importance of myth and ritual in bringing us into communion with a transcendent God.

Like politics and religion itself, each member of our congregations has an opinion about liturgy and often cherishes it intensely. For some, it's familiarity, while for others, it's a reflection of an especially important moment in their faith journey. And for still others, it's an appreciation of the rich history and tradition that have shaped liturgical expressions. Regardless of its source, these deeply held beliefs necessitate that the discussion of liturgy and changes to it—language, music, setting—be fostered by the clergy and vestry and include substantive conversations with the larger community. Although easily diverted by issues of personal preference and style, it's incumbent on congregational leaders that the focus remains on facilitating a shared (not solely individual) encounter with the holy. In pursuing this objective, the understanding of the meaning and function of sacrifice in liturgical celebration, as well as the complementary roles of the clergy and priesthood of all believers, are crucial. So, too, is the use of prayer to reflect our relationship with God, most notably through Jesus Christ, our Lord. Finally, it's essential that the discussions of liturgy be fully grounded in the Biblical narrative expressed through the rituals it embodies. May the Spirit continue to so move us to constantly explore the celebration of all that God is with reverence and joy.

Vestry Discussion

- Maurice counsels against the idolatry of liturgy. Is this manifest in your parish? If so, how?
- What might the clergy and vestry do to facilitate an even more faithful and healthier perspective on worship and liturgy?
- How does liturgical worship impact your faith, life, and relationships?
- In addition to liturgical worship, where and how do you most regularly encounter the holy? How do you respond?

Something to Ponder

From the King James Version of the Bible, the translation of 1 Chronicles 16.29b to "worship the Lord in the beauty of holiness" has shaped Christian liturgy, art, architecture, and theology. You're invited to consider this phrase as you reflect on your personal experience, as well as the leadership of your congregation.

Giving Voice to Our Faith

Opening Prayer

God of wonder and joy: give voice to our faith in the hymns we share; deepen our understanding of the God they reflect; open our eyes through them to see the beauty of all creation, as well as the cares of the world; and in our song grant us the sure and certain assurance of life eternal. Adoring you with our singing, we pray in Jesus' Name. Amen.

A Quote for Your Consideration

What brings us to church every Sunday? For some, it's the majesty of God evoked by the space. For many, it's a preacher whose sermons either soar in grand rhetoric or penetrate the very depths of our souls. And still for others, it's programming for our children and youth and the ministries we lead in the community. I suspect, however, that overwhelmingly we share a heartfelt love for the music of the Church, especially her hymns. Their melodies can be as lilting as they are powerful. Their lyrics often recall memories from the most special moments of our lives. And the shared voices of the gathered faithful (even when slightly off key) remind us of the faith and worship we experience in community. As we reflect on the important role of the Church's hymns in our personal lives and that of the congregation we serve, you're invited to consider the following quotation generally attributed to St. Augustine. "He who sings, prays twice."

Leadership in Context

Years ago, I was in a meeting with the parish committee walking with me in my discernment for the priesthood when one of the members inquired about the source of my theology ... beyond the study of Scripture. I think she expected me to respond with classics from the Church Fathers, the Reformers, and contemporary scholars. But that was not the case. Without a moment's hesitation, I declared "the hymns of the Church." Since my earliest years, their tunes and language have reverberated in my head. I've hummed them while walking. I've sung them driving. And as I grew older, I studied them. Although Scripture still grounds my theology and I treasure the insights of those who've explored its meaning and application in the world we inhabit, the hymns of worship continue to breathe life into my faith and give joy to its celebration.

I do wonder, however, how much attention we regularly pay to the words we sing in church? Are we fully engaged with them or simply transfixed by melodies? How might we more fully appropriate the theology they impart in our worship, study, and prayer? To begin to explore the possibilities, an examination of several central Christian precepts offered in the Church's hymns could be especially helpful.

Our understanding of God, for example, is defined as Triune—one God reflected in three Persons: Creator, Redeemer, and Sanctifier. Grasping this almost incomprehensible reality and communicating it have challenged preachers since the dawn of Christianity. And truth be known, more than a few senior clergy have foisted Trinity Sunday sermons on their junior and unsuspecting colleagues. Yet Hymn #371 (1982), "Thou Whose Almighty Word," provides a succinct, beautiful, and accessible description of the Trinity:

> Thou whose almighty word chaos and darkness heard,
>   and took their flight;
> hear us we humbly pray, and, where the Gospel day,
> sheds not its glorious ray,
> let there be light!
>
> Thou who didst come to bring only thy redeeming
>   wing healing and sight,
> health to the sick in mind, sight to the inly blind
> now to all human-kind,
> let there be light!
>
> Spirit of truth and love, life-giving, holy Dove, speed
>   forth thy flight!
> move on the water's face bearing the gifts of grace, and,
> in earth's darkest place,
> let there be light!

> Holy and blessed Three, glorious Trinity, wisdom, love, might:
> boundless as ocean's tide, rolling in fullest pride,
> through the world far and wide, let there be light!

In baptism, we are marked as Christ's own forever and fully welcomed into his Body, the Church. Too frequently, however, we limit our understanding of this sacrament to the act itself—the pouring of water, anointing with oil, and blessing. But as our Baptismal Covenant with God unequivocally asserts, the initiation it confers is to be lived daily, a hope lovingly expressed in Hymn #490 (1982), "I Want to Walk as a Child of the Light":

> I want to walk as a child of the light,
> I want to follow Jesus.
> God sent the stars to give light to the world.
> The star of my life is Jesus.
>
> *Refrain*
> *In him there is no darkness at all.*
> *The night and the day are both alike.*
> *The Lamb is the light of the city of God.*
> *Shine in my heart, Lord Jesus.*
>
> I want to see the brightness of God.
> I want to look at Jesus.
> Clear sun of righteousness, shine on my path,
> and show me the way to the Father.
>
> *Refrain*

I'm looking for the coming of Christ.
I want to be with Jesus.
When we have run with patience the race,
we shall know the joy of Jesus.

Refrain

You would have thought that as the central act of Christian worship, the Eucharist would have evolved as straightforward, simple to understand, and absent controversy. However, despite the attempts of liturgical scholars to define and organize the actions that make the Eucharist, they remain the subject of ongoing debate. Also lacking a consensus within the Church is what constitutes the Real Presence in the Eucharist and how it's attained. And even an understanding of its purpose—memorial, remembrance, or sacrifice—remains contentious more than 2,000 years after its institution. Indeed, the Eucharist is imbued with mystery. So rather than attempting to dissect the complex anatomy of this sacrament, Hymn #304 (1982), "I Come with Joy to Meet My Lord," celebrates with the Anglican divine Richard Hooker the impact on those who participate in the Communion (2002):

> I come with joy to meet my Lord,
> forgiven, loved, and free,
> in awe and wonder to recall
> his life laid down for me.

> I come with Christians far and near
> to find, as all are fed,

> the new community of love
> in Christ's communion bread.
>
> As Christ breaks bread and bids us share,
> each proud division ends.
> That love that made us makes us one,
> and strangers now are friends.
>
> And thus with joy we greet our Lord.
> His presence, always near,
> is in such friendship better known:
> we see and praise him here.
>
> Together met, together bound,
> we'll go our different ways,
> and as his people in the world
> we'll live and speak his praise.

Clearly, the Eucharist summons us to a life of Christian faith and discipleship, the dimensions of which are virtually boundless. Regardless of the context for ministry or its articulation, however, implicit in the Eucharist is the recognition that following Christ is a daily challenge that can only be met through God's infinite grace and mercy, as given voice in Hymn #686 (1982), "Come Thou Font of Every Blessing."

> Come thou font of every blessing, tune my heart to sing thy grace!
> streams of mercy never ceasing, call for songs of loudest praise.

Teach me some melodious sonnet, sung by flaming
   tongues above.
Praise the mount! Oh, fix me on it, mount of God's
   unchanging love.

Here I find my greatest treasure; hither, by thy help, I've
   come;
and I hope, by thy good pleasure, safely to arrive at home,
Jesus sought me when a stranger wandering from the
   fold of God;
he, to rescue me from danger, interposed his precious
   blood.

Oh, to grace how great a debtor daily I'm constrained to
   be! Let thy goodness, like a fetter, bind my wandering
   heart to thee:
Prone to wander Lord, I feel it, prone to leave the God
   I love;
Here's my heart, oh, take and seal it, seal it for thy
   courts above.

Finally, in this brief survey of theology and faith conveyed through hymns, we're reminded that our lives and ministry play out in community, in the Body of Christ—the Church. Although Scripture, the work of centuries of scholars, and hymns across many different traditions offer various descriptions of the Church—militant, universal, and triumphant, for example—"How Lovely Is Thy Dwelling Place," Hymn #517 (1982) conveys an invitation and warmth especially alluring:

How lovely is thy dwelling-place, O lord of hosts, to me!
My thirsty soul desires and longs within thy courts to be;
my very heart and flesh cry out,
O living God, for thee.

Beside thine altars, gracious Lord, the swallows find a nest;
how happy they who dwell with thee and praise the without rest;
and happy they whose hearts are set
upon the pilgrim's quest.

They who go through the dessert vale will find it filled with springs,
and they shall climb from height to height till Zion's temple rings
with praise to thee, in glory throned,
Lord God, great King of kings.

One day within thy courts excels a thousand spent away;
How happy they who keep thy laws nor from thy precepts stray,
for thou shalt surely bless all those
who live the words they pray."

Although barely a cursory examination of the theology embedded in our hymns, this discussion nonetheless reveals their almost inexhaustible potential for spiritual formation and growth. Whether the familiar songs of Sunday school or the many we sing during worship, the hymns of the Church provide a provocative context for exploring the faith we share and its nuances. It's easy to imagine, for example, classes for children and adults that ground theological discussion in these hymns. So too might we incorporate them into our personal and communal prayers. But most important, we hope that even as we sing these hymns, they transport us into the presence of the Divine. Indeed, "Let us sing to the Lord; let us make a joyful noise to the rock of our salvation" (Psalm 95.1)!

Vestry Discussion

- How do the hymns of the Church or other religious music function in your spiritual life?
- Do you spend time specifically reflecting on these hymns, what they convey, and how they might deepen your faith? If not, why not?
- What ways might your parish use hymns and music to broaden faith formation?
- Might hymn singing become an outreach ministry of your congregation?

Something to Ponder

As I prepared this reflection, I was reminded of those hymns I especially treasure, foremost among them Hymn #460 (1982), "Alleluia, Sing to Jesus." It's been sung at several of the most joyful and painful moments of my life, for which I am deeply grateful. You're invited to consider a "favorite hymn" and to let its words roll in your mind and melody ride on your breath.

Put Your Money Where Your Faith Is

Opening Prayer

God of unlimited abundance, boundless grace, and compassion beyond measure, grant us clarity of vision and mission and the trust to commit our financial resources to achieving them. Send your Spirit to empower us to act boldly and responsibly, to manage wisely, and to lead with faith and conviction. Bless our work for the life of the world, in Jesus' Name. Amen.

A Quote for Your Consideration

Fiscal responsibility is essential to the effective governance of any organization, including a church. A realistic budget broadly supported by the vestry and congregation is the primary tool for expressing their priorities in the context of the church's vision, mission, and values. Equally as important is the budget's ability to provide the guidance necessary to manage the church's assets in an ever-changing environment. The following quote from eighteenth-century Anglican divine William Law (2002) challenges us to "put our money where our faith is":

> If a man had eyes and hands and feet that he could give to those that needed them, if he should either lock them up in a chest or please himself with some needless or ridiculous use of them instead of giving them to his brethren that were blind and lame, should we not justly reckon him an inhuman wretch? If he should rather choose to amuse himself with furnishing

his house with those things than to entitle himself to an eternal reward by giving them to those that needed eyes and hands, might we not justly reckon him mad? Now money has very much the nature of eyes and feet. If we either lock it up in chests or waste it in needless or ridiculous ornaments of apparel, while others are starving in nakedness, we are not far from the cruelty of him that chooses rather to adorn his house with the hands and eyes than to give them to those that need them.

Leadership in Context

Decades ago, the late Sr. Mary Roch Rocklage, RSM, chair of the board of Mercy Health in St. Louis and subsequently chair of the American Hospital Association, was engaged in a testy debate with health-care advocates who decried the profits of local hospitals. They called into question their commitment to those who couldn't afford care, shouting, "No mission, no margin." Sr. Roch heard them, paused, and then gave them a quick lesson in the sad reality of health care in the United States, responding, "No margin, no mission." Although a champion of the charitable ministry of hospitals (especially not-for-profits), she also understood the necessity of rigorously managing both revenues and expenses to ensure the ongoing capacity to provide health care to all who need it.

Whether in hospitals, "mom and pop shops," large corporations, or churches, fiscal responsibility requires constant attention and the coordination of several key processes. A realistic budget "owned" by the entire organization has already been noted as the foundation for managing resources—financial, capital, and human. However, it's only a start. Transparent financial statements, regular monitoring by the vestry, and routine audits are also essential. Financial policies and controls that minimize the potential for misuse, fraud, or theft are equally critical in safeguarding the church's assets and protecting those with access to funds. Too often given inadequate attention, however, is the vestry's responsibility for the stewardship of both financial investments and the ministries they sustain. The Gospel of Matthew (25.14–28) speaks directly to this point.

> For it is as if a man, going on a journey, summoned his slaves and entrusted his property to them; to one he gave five talents, to another two, to another one, to each according to his ability. Then he went away. The one who had received the five talents went off at once and traded with them and made five more talents. In the same way, the one who had the two talents made two more talents. But the one who had received the one talent went off and dug a hole in the ground and hid his master's money. After a long time the master of those slaves came and settled accounts with them. Then the one who had received the five talents came forward, bringing five more talents, saying, "Master, you handed over to me five talents; see, I have made five more talents." His master said to him, "Well done, good and trustworthy slave; you have been trustworthy in a few things; I will put you in charge of many things; enter into the joy of your

master." And the one with the two talents also came forward, saying, "Master, you handed over to me two talents; see, I have made two more talents." His master said to him, "Well done, good and trustworthy slave; you have been trustworthy in a few things; I will put you in charge of many things; enter into the joy of your master." Then the one who had received the one talent also came forward, saying, "Master, I knew that you were a harsh man, reaping where you did not sow, and gathering where you did not scatter seed; so I was afraid, and I went and hid your talent in the ground. Here you have what is yours." But his master replied, "You wicked and lazy slave! You knew, did you, that I reap where I did not sow and gather where I did not scatter? Then you ought to have invested my money with the bankers, and on my return I would have received what was my own with interest. So take the talent from him, and give it to the one with the ten talents."

This well-known parable appears in distinct forms that occasion different interpretations in the Gospels of Matthew and Luke. This iteration, however, specifically addresses what it means to be a "good and trustworthy" servant. Importantly, New Testament scholar M. Eugene Boring (1995) argues that such faithful discipleship "is not mere theological correctness, passive waiting, or strict obedience to clear instructions, but active responsibility that takes initiative and risk."

For vestries, the implication is clear. "Living within its means" is not the sole expectation of a congregation. Rather as Matthew's parable pointedly projects, we're challenged to expand our vision for ministry and invest wisely to support this new work. No doubt, we'll experience both success and failure, but as Boring noted, we need to take the "initiative and risk" to extend the Gospel—with our funds, our witness to the world, and our labor.

Vestry Discussion

- How do you understand the role of the vestry in stewarding our congregation's financial, capital, and human resources?
- In deliberations about finances, what is your priority—mission or margin?
- How should your vestry manage financial risk, as well as the risks associated with new initiatives?

Something to Ponder

Key to our understanding of the stewardship of the congregation's resources is how to grow them within an acceptable level of risk and uncertainty. Therefore, you're encouraged to reflect on "investment" as an essential strategy to achieving this goal.

Channeling Our Best Intentions

Opening Prayer

God of infinite love, mercy beyond measure, and unbridled compassion: look with favor on those whose lives have suffered for want of even the most basic of physical and emotional sustenance; open our hearts with generosity and wisdom in the care we share with them; ensure that our charity embraces the dignity of all whose lives we touch; grant us a selfless spirit; and envelop our work in hope. For the sake of your Son, we pray. Amen.

A Quote for Your Consideration

Central to the life of a congregation and its ministry among one another, as well as its engagement with the larger community, is the care of those who cannot provide for their own needs either temporarily or chronically—food, housing, health care, and clothing, to name only a few. Faith communities of all traditions have a long and storied history of service to the poor and marginalized, one also too often plagued by self-serving motives, horrendous personal abuse, and financial scandal. The challenge we face is to channel "the better angels of our nature" in ways that honestly and without judgment embrace the reality of the human condition and work tirelessly to elevate it. However, as twentieth-century Archbishop of Canterbury William Temple (2002a) so pointedly remarked, we're equally called to contest the very injustices that create and sustain a social order that necessitates charity:

> If the present order is taken for granted or assumed to be sacrosanct, charity from the more or less fortunate would seem virtuous and commendable; to those for whom the order itself is suspect or worse, such charity is blood-money. Why should some be in the position to dispense and others to need that kind of charity?

Leadership in Context

In his scathing indictment of often misguided and self-aggrandizing charity, Robert Lupton (2011) describes foreign mission trips with different church groups painting the same building multiple times in a year, construction following hurricanes at ten times the local cost and depriving residents of essential work, and the humiliation of fathers unable to provide gifts for their children at Christmas as toys are brought to their homes by "the more fortunate." Based on his four decades of experience in community organizing and serving the neediest throughout the United States as well as internationally, he has proposed *The Oath for Compassionate Service*:

- Never do for the poor what they have (or could have) the capacity to do for themselves.
- Limit one-way giving to emergency situations.
- Strive to empower the poor through employment, lending, and investing, using grants sparingly to reinforce achievements.
- Subordinate self-interests to the needs of those being served.
- Listen closely to those you seek to help, especially to what is not being said—unspoken feelings may contain essential clues to effective service.
- Above all, do no harm.

Lupton's is largely a strategy of accompaniment in the fulfillment of the charitable work in which faith communities are engaged. It encourages us to partner with those we seek to help, listen to and trust them, and empower them to develop the resources necessary to elevate their lives supplemented with carefully targeted resources we can offer. In essence, he seeks to balance the depth of our compassion and mercy with the wisdom gained from experience.

Certainly, there are elements of truth embedded in Lupton's principles, and many (if not most) of us who've worked with the poor and marginalized can attest to their importance in framing charitable service. Nevertheless, they need to be interpreted in the context of the mental health, housing, and addiction status of specific individuals and the social systems that impede aid. Additionally, efforts are frequently undermined by woefully inappropriate assumptions about poverty and those whose lives are daily impacted by it, for example, the work ethic of the poor, the availability of resources that can be secured without charitable assistance, and what truly constitutes an emergency. "Lazy" . . . "Pull yourself up by your own bootstraps" . . . and "Your failure to plan is not my emergency" too frequently are echoed in discussions of who deserves our charitable largess and how it should be delivered. Despite our tendency toward kindness, the biases of privilege regularly and sometimes subconsciously cloud our vision, undermine our relationships with individuals and communities in need of our care, and limit the potential for sustainable success. How, then, might we recast Lupton's principles (which have much to commend them) in a way that respects the dignity and agency of the poor, challenges systems that perpetuate poverty, and is grounded in the Gospel?

Jesus himself seems to accept a social and economic structure rooted in "haves" and "have nots," with Matthew quoting him, saying, "For you will always have the poor with you, but you will not always have me" (26.11). However, his comment was not intended as the legitimization of class distinctions but a rejoinder to his disciples who had questioned the use of an expensive ointment by an unnamed woman to anoint him rather than selling it to raise funds for the poor. In fact, as Archbishop Temple implores us, we're first and foremost to pray relentlessly and advocate tirelessly for policies, strategies, and actions that liberate the poor from an economic caste system and eliminate the institutionalized factors that enable it.

The Hebrew Scriptures' book of First Samuel also reminds us that the dignity of the poor is fundamental to our response to their needs:

> He raises up the poor from the dust; he lifts the needy from the ash heap to make them sit with princes and inherit a seat of honor. For the pillars of the earth are the Lord's, and on them he has set the world (2.8).

The New Testament Letter of James (2.5–7) echoes the same sentiment.

> Listen, my beloved brothers and sisters. Has not God chosen the poor in the world to be rich in faith and to be heirs of the kingdom that he has promised to those who love him? But you have dishonored the poor. Is it not the rich who oppress you? Is it not they who drag you into court? Is it not they

who blaspheme the excellent name that was invoked over you?

Both passages speak to the inherent worth of all God's family and, as such, demand that we abandon generalized, unsubstantiated assumptions about the poor derived from our own ignorance and prejudices. They require that even as we reach out to communities, we seek to meet individuals with unique circumstances, needs, and sensitivities to the help we offer. And we're asked to accept that the perspective on an emergency is best understood by the person experiencing it, not those of us living amid comfort and plenty.

Although empowering the poor with innovative economic strategies is critical to dismantling poverty, they must be rooted in the spirit of abundance and generosity encouraged in the Torah:

> If there is among you anyone in need, a member of your community in any of your towns within the land that the Lord your God is giving you, do not be hard-hearted or tight-fisted toward your needy neighbor. You should rather open your hand, willingly lending enough to meet the need, whatever it may be. Be careful that you do not entertain a mean thought, thinking, "The seventh year, the year of remission, is near," and therefore view your needy neighbor with hostility and give nothing; your neighbor might cry to the Lord against you, and you would incur guilt. Give liberally and be ungrudging when you do so, for on this account the Lord your

God will bless you in all your work and in all that you undertake. Since there will never cease to be some in need on the earth, I therefore command you, "Open your hand to the poor and needy neighbor in your land" (Deuteronomy 15.7–11).

That charity cannot be authentic absent the subjugation of our self-interests is generically asserted in Lupton's principles but, in the context of faith, reflects specific service to God. The Hebrew Scriptures' Book of Proverbs, for example, emphasizes that, "Whoever is kind to the poor lends to the Lord and will be repaid in full" (19.17).

To be sure, the temptation to respond immediately to the crises we observe in our communities and around the world can be overwhelming. We ache as others suffer, we're certain that resources can be marshaled, and we understand that time is often of the essence. Nevertheless, our perception of the problem, as well as the needs of others, is often distorted by our own experience and beliefs, with a well-intentioned but hasty response actually damaging relationships and the potential for success. Again, we're reminded in the Letter of James (1.19), "You must understand this, my beloved: let everyone be quick to listen, slow to speak..."

The vestry's leadership in framing a parish's charitable ministry, as well as managing the human, financial, and institutional resources dedicated to it, is essential to living a faith that is genuine, respectful, responsive, and truly focused on the needs of the most vulnerable among us. Adopting a statement of principles to guide decision-making, sharing it with the larger congregation, and consistently using it in the evaluation of charitable opportunities will both facilitate and enhance this vital aspect of Christian service. In doing so, we join in the language of the Book of Common Prayer (1979) asking that God, "Grant us grace that we may honor you with our substance, and, remembering the account which we must one day give, may be faithful stewards of your bounty."

Vestry Discussion

- How do the perceptions of the "deserving" and "undeserving" poor shape your understanding of charity and your congregation's response to those in need?
- What systemic factors inhibit successful outreach to and empowerment of the poor? How might they be diminished?
- What is your personal commitment to charitable work and how do you actualize it?
- What do communities of faith uniquely bring (if anything) to charitable work? How best might their perspective be integrated with secular initiatives?

Something to Ponder

For many, our personal experience being poor or engaging with those who are is limited or non-existent. This lack of familiarity, systemic prejudice, economic segregation, and a deeply rooted belief in self-reliance contribute substantially to our largely ineffective responses to poverty and too frequently a lack of genuine empathy. As you reflect on how you and your congregation embrace charitable ministry, you're invited to consider the ancient proverb, "Give a man a fish and feed him for a day. Teach him how to fish and feed him for a lifetime." Then, ask yourself, "How do you know he really wants fish?"

Violence in Our Midst

Opening Prayer

God of all mercy, who knows our insecurities, our isolation, and our pain: comfort the abandoned; lift the souls of all in despair; and open the hearts of those who care for them; in the name of the God who embraces all who feel alone. Amen.

A Quote for Your Consideration

It's not surprising that the concept of "sanctuary"—space made holy by the worship engaged within it—has evolved more broadly to reflect the peace, serenity, and safety it affords. Not only does it provide comfort and the opportunity to commune with the Divine, but it also offers security for those fleeing political and religious oppression, domestic abuse, and threats to their lives. Yet, these sacred spaces also have been the site of some of the most horrendous murders in recent history—Pittsburgh's Tree of Life Synagogue, First Baptist Church in Sutherland Springs, Texas, and Emanuel African American Episcopal Church in Charleston, South Carolina, to name only a few.

These tragedies share the common element of an external threat—an aggrieved lone shooter otherwise unattached to the congregation. In response, many houses of worship have added armed security and restricted access to their facilities. Far too frequently ignored, however, is the reality of violence in the very midst of our faith communities. Although most will never experience a mass shooting, for example, many will likely be touched at some point in time by the most prevalent form of gun violence: suicide. Nor are congregations and their members immune from the effects of domestic abuse and bullying. Consequently, providing a safe environment, identifying those at risk for violence, and ensuring the infrastructure necessary to support victims and confront and care for perpetrators are essential to the leadership of clergy and their vestry partners.

Although the causes of violence are many, a sense of alienation often seems to be at the root. Human rights activist and philanthropist Martin Luther King III speaks to just this point, observing: "Violence is the language of the unheard." As we consider the violence in our midst and our response to it, creating a safe space for those at risk, as well as one in which troubled souls might be heard, embraced, and loved, is imperative if we're to achieve the hope of becoming a beloved community.

Leadership in Context

In his magisterial work, *The Better Angels of Our Nature: Why Violence Has Declined*, Stephen Pinker (2012) argues convincingly that lethal violence has dramatically decreased over the course of recorded history, predominantly because of the rise of nation states and their ability to control the resources necessary to wage war. Domestically, despite pervasive media accounts that would suggest a nation overwhelmed by violence, Patrick Sharkey (2018) has documented a sharp decline in violent crimes in recent decades. Nevertheless, we remain a society in which violence too often breaks into our lives and devastates so many.

No social institution is immune from its trauma—not manufacturing plants, post offices, schools, hospitals, or churches. Each has the responsibility to assess its risks and implement initiatives to limit them. As a community of faith dedicated to ministering to all—the victims and perpetrators of violence alike—we first need to understand the specific violence most likely to emerge in our congregations.

No form of violence has been more tolerated and condoned—let alone encouraged—than the abuse of women by the men in their lives. The prevalence of domestic violence is staggering. Twenty-five percent of women will be severely physically abused in their lifetime, with more than 1,500 women killed annually by a current or former intimate partner. And approximately half of all women will be psychologically or emotionally abused by an intimate partner at some time in their life. In addition to the survivors themselves, more than 15 million children witness acts of domestic violence annually (Smith 2020).

Mistakenly, discussions of domestic and sexualized violence often are cast exclusively in the context of heterosexual relationships in which the male is the perpetrator. However, more than 14% of men will be abused during their lifetime. In addition, 40% of lesbian and 60% of bisexual women, as well as 25% of gay and 33% of bisexual men, will be physically assaulted, stalked, or raped at some time during their lives. And tragically, 50% of transgender individuals will experience sexual violence during their lives (Smith 2020).

The bullying of youth and the workplace harassment and "mobbing" of adults pose additional challenges for faith communities. Not only are they rampant across society, but it also seems reasonable to assume that they occur within our congregational walls. Among 12–18-year-olds in a recent study, 21% reported being bullied by schoolmates at least once during the year—the prevalence of which is likely to rise significantly with increases in cyber-bullying. Likewise, almost one-third of adults report being bullied in their workplace or other group settings (Smith 2020).

Domestic violence, sexualized abuse, and youth and adult bullying share the commonality of victim and perpetrator, and, in the context of our parish life, both may be active in the congregation. In the aftermath of the sex abuse scandals that plagued several Christian denominations during the past several decades, it's heartening to note the number of mandated "safe people" training programs for clergy and lay leaders (including vestries) that have been implemented. Nevertheless, it's far too easy to assume that training will eliminate the potential for inappropriate behavior and, if it occurs, "the rector will deal with it."

The reality, however, is that we are community bound with one another through Jesus Christ. Consequently, we share the responsibility for understanding the signs of abuse and bullying, being attentive to them, and ensuring that clergy, mental health professionals, and, when necessary, law enforcement officials are engaged. We also share the development of appropriate intervention strategies and the ongoing pastoral care of victims, as well as perpetrators. While hopefully infrequent, congregational leaders would be well-served to anticipate these forms of violence and to plan for a reasoned, thoughtful, and loving response that includes the opportunity for both accountability and reconciliation.

Suicide is the act of an individual often borne of depression, social isolation, and the absence of hope. Nevertheless, it occurs in the context of community—a family, school, or church. And while members of these social networks would not generally be considered perpetrators, they can be enablers through their actions (or lack) toward the person at risk. Sadly, the rate of suicide nationally has grown dramatically since 2000, now approaching 14/100,000 population. More than 1.6 million Americans attempt to take their own lives annually, and 49,000 succeed (Centers for Disease Control 2024).

So prevalent is suicide, it's likely that many of our congregations and their members have been touched by it. Consequently, it's important for clergy and the entire congregation to be attentive to the warning signs of suicidal ideation—an expressed desire to die, feelings of being a burden, hopelessness, unbearable physical or emotional pain, and depression among them. Ensuring that an appropriate mental health referral network is in place, educating the parish, and supporting the person in crisis and caregivers are essential. And especially important is the need to wrap the survivors of a life lost to suicide in Jesus' embrace through the congregation's love and ministry.

Certainly, the care of the victims of violence, their perpetrators, and those at risk for suicide requires the skills of trained pastoral, mental health, and criminal justice professionals. Nevertheless, vestries should make it a priority to be well-informed and ensure that the necessary educational resources and emotional support are available to the congregation.

Indeed, we're reminded in the Letter to the Colossians (3.12–17) of the sacred duty of the Church in our care for all in need, especially those at risk for or who have suffered violence:

> As God's chosen ones, holy and beloved, clothe yourselves with compassion, kindness, humility, meekness, and patience. Bear with one another and, if anyone has a complaint against another, forgive each other; just as the Lord has forgiven you, so you also must forgive. Above all, clothe yourselves with love, which binds everything together in perfect harmony. And let the peace of Christ rule in your hearts, to which indeed you were called in the one body. And be thankful. Let the word of Christ dwell in you richly; teach and admonish one another in all wisdom; and with gratitude in your hearts sing psalms, hymns, and spiritual songs to God. And whatever you do, in word or deed, do everything in the name of the Lord Jesus, giving thanks to God the Father through him.

A more detailed discussion of violence and the church's response to it is presented in the author's six-session multimedia curriculum, *Each Other's Keeper: The Church's Response to Violence,* published in 2020 by Forward Movement's ChurchNext and the Episcopal Diocese of Missouri.

Vestry Discussion

- Has your life been touched by violence? If so, how did you cope with it? Was your faith community helpful and supportive?
- Do you believe that the members of your congregation are potentially subject to violence and that the congregation has a responsibility to intervene whenever appropriate?
- Have your congregation or its members experienced violence? If so, how did you respond? What did you learn from the experience?
- Have you developed an infrastructure within your congregation to identify potential or real violence within your midst, respond to it, and care for both victims and perpetrators? If not, why? If so, how is it functioning?

Something to Ponder

We live in a world in which violence in its many different forms permeates our daily lives. The Church is not immune, nor are our members. As we consider our responsibility to care for each other in the most difficult of times, you're encouraged to reflect on "sanctuary" and how we embrace it in the life we share.

When Things "Go off the Rails"

Opening Prayer

Almighty God, who guides and sustains us even in the most trying of times: watch over our parish family as we work to understand each other; bridge our differences; heal our wounds; forgive our anger; and reconcile us as we live into our call as the Body of Christ. Grant us patience, love, kindness, and wisdom as we lead this congregation through turbulent waters. All this we humbly pray in Jesus' Name. Amen.

A Quote for Your Consideration

Life in community is difficult—whether as a family, in an organization, or as members of a church. Despite our shared goals and commitment to the work in which we're engaged, things occasionally "go off the rails," all too often resulting in fractured relationships and collective dysfunction. As leaders of our congregation, how do we begin to understand the full dimensions of conflict within our midst, repair damaged bonds, and move faithfully to restore our focus and ministry? Reflecting on this challenge, you're invited to consider the following quote from twentieth-century Anglican bishop and leader of the East African revival movement Festo Kivengere (2002):

> No one ever forgives without suffering. It costs to forgive. And costs dearly. That God forgives is a divine miracle. The power of his justice and his mercy working in harmony, restoring the alienated

wrongdoer, is the heart of "the good news of God." Mercy is not the opposite of justice, injustice is, and God has nothing to do with injustice in his central work of liberating the guilty through his reconciling love. The price of reconciliation is full identification with the guilty in order to arouse hope for liberation and restoration.

Leadership in Context

Even the healthiest of churches are not immune to crises. Clergy engage in improper behavior with parishioners, staff abscond with funds, "liturgical wars" envelop congregations, and ministries to the most vulnerable go awry. Some crises are legal or ecclesiastical and must be resolved by the appropriate judicial authorities. Others are significant disruptions to the integrity and stability of the local faith community that need a pastoral and therapeutic response that acknowledges people's pain and structures a conversation that fosters mutually acceptable solutions and reconciles opposing parties. In either case, the Body of Christ has been assaulted, and the focus of congregational leaders must be on re-establishing organizational and personal relationships that will enable the parish to move forward with its mission and ministries.

Although each situation will present unique circumstances, crisis intervention theory (CIT) proposes several sequential steps essential to understanding and resolving crises. First is the recognition that both individuals and organizations generally inhabit a stable environment (homeostasis), and crises upend usual functioning. Normal relationships and coping strategies are challenged and frequently fail amid incidents seemingly beyond control.

Recognizing the specific type of instability created by a particular crisis also is essential. CIT theorists have proffered four dimensions: (1) *intrapersonal*, which compromises individual coping mechanisms; (2) *interpersonal*, which limits communication and participation problems solving; (3) *physical*, which arises from concern over individual health and well-being; and (4) *spiritual*, which calls into question the redemptive quality of God or value of the faith community. These dimensions are not mutually exclusive, although one typically is dominant. However, what is crucial in resolving a crisis is accurately identifying the dimension(s) involved (Pavelsky 2005).

The third step in crisis intervention is recognizing its specific cause and expression. For example, does a clergy dispute with the vestry emanate from a loss of control, a loss of support, or a new situation—and, from whose perspective?

Developing a model for returning to individual or organizational stability and an actionable plan to implement it is the penultimate step in the process, followed by the final stage, which monitors and regularly assesses progress in resolving the crisis and moving forward.

Although CIT provides a framework for addressing the multiple dimensions of crisis and conflict within a faith community, St. Paul (Ephesians 4.25–5.2) offers instruction for the behaviors we're to engage as we work to confront difficult and tense situations, change disruptive conduct, heal real and perceived wounds, and reclaim the ministry to which we've been called:

> So then, putting away falsehood, let all of us speak the truth to our neighbors, for we are members of one another. Be angry but do not sin; do not let the sun go down on your anger, and do not make room for the devil. Thieves must give up stealing; rather, let them labor and work honestly with their own hands, so as to have something to share with the needy. Let no evil talk come out of your mouths, but only what is useful for building up, as there is need, so that your words may give grace to those who hear. And do not grieve the Holy Spirit of God, with which you were marked with a seal for the day of redemption. Put away from you all bitterness and wrath and anger and wrangling and slander, together with all malice, and be kind to one another, tenderhearted, forgiving one another, as God in Christ has forgiven you. Therefore be imitators of God, as beloved children, and live in love, as Christ loved us and gave himself up for us, a fragrant offering and sacrifice to God.

Paul offers wise counsel for the Church, as well as secular organizations, when conflicts arise, tempers flare, and confrontations all too often become personal. His exhortations remind us to ground our discussions in truth—not innuendo, uncorroborated accusations, or outright falsehoods. We're not to hold grudges, speak evil of others, or offend the Spirit through whom God's grace has been made known. And we're to turn away from malice, backroom maneuvering, and slandering those with whom we disagree, however strongly. Rather, we're to approach the resolution of even the most embittered situations with love, kindness, charity, and the forgiveness so fully shared with us by God through Christ Jesus. Even and especially in crises, Paul challenges us to be "imitators of God, as beloved children" (Ephesians 5.1).

Vestry Discussion

- What important lessons have you learned from crises you've faced in your leadership of the congregation or in your personal life?
- Should the congregation have a crisis intervention plan and, if so, what generic issues should it address, and what should be the role of the vestry?
- What might be established within the congregation to help identify and resolve contentious issues before they become crises?

Something to Ponder

It's almost inevitable that a congregation will be confronted by a crisis at some point in time. Depending on its internal chemistry, mission, and ministry, a faith community may find itself more frequently challenged. Regardless, it's imperative that a vestry anticipate the likelihood of a crisis and develop a process for responding to it. You're invited to consider what it means to "prepare" both the vestry and parish for crises.

Clergy Taking Leave

Opening Prayer

God of unbounded presence and grace, we rejoice in the ministry of pastors who have inspired us, challenged us, humbled us, taught us, heard us, moved us, laughed with us, cried with us, comforted us, prayed with us, sang with us, lifted us up in faith, and given us hope. Bless beloved priests as they take leave to serve new cures. Send your Spirit to inspire their leadership, empower their preaching, strengthen their courage, and extend their love. All in Jesus' Name we pray. Amen.

A Quote for Your Consideration

We regularly say "Goodbye" to priests who take their leave to begin new cures with other congregations. For those of us who remain, it's generally a time mixed with joy, sadness, hope, and uncertainty. However, as we prepare to bid clergy farewell, we're also mindful that they will have much work to do in their new parishes and will need our continued prayers for their ministries. Seventeenth-century Anglican priest and theologian Jeremy Taylor invites us to join these priests in praying for the journey ahead (2002):

> O Almighty God, Father and Lord of all the creatures, by secret and undiscernible ways bringing good out of evil; give me wisdom from above; teach me to be content in all changes of person and condition, to be temperate in prosperity, and in adversity to be meek,

patient, and resigned; and to look through the cloud, in the meantime doing my duty with an unwearied diligence, and an undisturbed resolution, laying up my hopes in heaven and the rewards of holy living, and being strengthened with the spirit of the inner man, through Jesus Christ our Lord. Amen.

Leadership in Context

Clergy come and go. It's the reality of life in the Church. In fact, the average congregational tenure of an Episcopal priest is only five years. Some retire, others transition to new ministries, some are forced out of their current position by local conflict, and still others leave ordained life behind.

Regardless of the circumstances, however, both priests and their former congregants grapple with the loss of relationships, their shared successes and failures, and uncertain futures. Significant attention has been given to clergy transitions and the sense of grief that follows them. Less examined have been our hopes and expectations for each other as we move forward.

Undeniably, no one in Scripture has more experience with "taking leave" and commenting on it than St. Paul, ministering to communities throughout the Roman Empire for decades. As he prepared to depart from the church in Colossae in the Province of Asia, for example, he exhorted the congregation to remain diligent in their faith but also requested their prayers that he might be freed from prison to continue to proclaim the Gospel:

> Devote yourselves to prayer, keeping alert in it with thanksgiving. At the same time, pray for us as well, that God will open to us a door for the word, that we may declare the mystery of Christ, for which I am prison, so that I may reveal it clearly, as I should (Colossians 4.2–4).

Similarly, Paul called for vigilance as he wrote to the church in Rome, stating, "I urge you, brothers and sisters, to keep an eye on those who cause dissensions and offenses, in opposition to the teaching that you have learned; avoid them" (Romans 16.17). And yet in another leave-taking, he asks for prayers in support of his ministry even as he summons continued faithfulness from the Thessalonians:

> Finally, brothers and sisters, pray for us, so that the word of the Lord may spread rapidly and be glorified everywhere, just as it is among you, and that we may be rescued from wicked and evil people, for not all have faith. But the Lord is faithful; he will strengthen you and guard you from the evil one. And we have confidence in the Lord concerning you, that you are doing and will go on doing the things that we command. May the Lord direct your hearts to the love of God and to the steadfastness of Christ (2 Thessalonians 3.1–5).

Several themes emerge from these examples of St. Paul's frequent pastoral transitions. First, he leaves a message for those he's been serving, specifically to remain faithful in prayer and gratitude, as well as mindful of those who might seek to disrupt the community. While prodding them, he also expresses full trust in their ongoing discipleship. Second, as he remembers those he served, so too does Paul ask that they hold him in prayer that he might be free to proclaim the Good News without impediment.

As we prepare for the departure of clergy at some point in time, Paul's exhortations would serve us well. To be sure, there will be time to ponder the loss and grief. But even more important, we're invited to look toward and celebrate the future—encouraging them in a new ministry, praying for the voice they will bring to a different community, and extending hope for every success. Likewise, may we who remain warmly accept the blessings of those who have served us so well and so selflessly. And may our work in the years ahead honor the gifts they have willingly shared and nurtured among us.

Vestry Discussion

- How can we best support our clergy during their leave-taking and in their new cures?
- What are the boundaries that should surround our support?
- As a vestry, how can we assist the congregation in creating the space necessary to transition clergy leaders?

Something to Ponder

It's customary for priests who have left their cures to abstain from contact with former congregants for some time (usually one to two years) and, subsequently, only engage in it with the express permission of the incumbent rector and diocesan bishop. To be sure, exceptions can and should be made when the circumstances warrant it. Nevertheless, establishing a clear demarcation between the ministry of the past and that of the present is fundamental to ensuring the healthy transition of pastoral leadership for both priests and parishioners. In this context, you're invited to consider the concept of "boundary" as you prepare to shepherd your congregation through the eventual time in which you welcome a new rector and are discouraged from communication with the immediate predecessor.

"Peace"—Welcoming Clergy

Opening Prayer

O God of hospitality and grace, who invites us into the full presence of the Divine through baptism and the Eucharist: bless our congregation with the spirit of welcome to all; a consciousness of those in need; loving hearts and hands to serve them; and a profound sense of joy and gratitude as disciples of Jesus, the Christ. In whose Name we pray. Amen.

A Quote for Your Consideration

Just as we bid farewell to clergy so too do we welcome them, and, in doing so, our attention is drawn to what it means to truly extend hospitality to a new leader in our midst. How do we prepare ourselves, the vestry that will share leadership with the rector, and a congregation anticipating the excitement of new directions even as we maintain and strengthen the ministries our congregation has long engaged? Although there are many ways to extend our welcome, you're invited to consider the following quote from Episcopalian storyteller and author Madeleine L'Engle (2002) as she grounds hospitality as an expression of our faith. "Virtue is not the sign of a Christian. Joy is."

Leadership in Context

Welcoming is among the most fundamental of our interactions with the world around us. It's the warmth of openness to friend and stranger alike. It's the wisp of surprise greeting something new—a change of seasons, the salt in the air as we approach the ocean, the strike of trout rising to the first hatch of spring. And it's the specific gestures we use to express our welcome—handshakes, fist bumps, hugs, high fives, and kisses, among others.

Each of these dimensions of hospitality will be at the forefront of the welcome of new clergy. This is not merely the embrace of the latest organizational leader with pleasantries, a reception, and dinner. While hopefully genuine, these reflect society's sense of propriety and etiquette. However, more—much more—is expected of faith communities as they greet those who will lead and shepherd them. At the very core is Jesus' outpouring when he first encountered the disciples following His resurrection: "Peace be with you" (John 20.19b).

In various forms and with different emphases, "peace" has been an essential element of hospitality and welcome among

God's faithful. The *shalom* of ancient Israel conveyed a sense of wholeness marked by well-being, prosperity, justice, and God's triumph over demonic forces and raging chaos—attributes enjoyed individually and by the community, as well as extended as a blessing to welcome others.

The New Testament's use of *eirene* expands the Hebrew *shalom* to include an inner peace grounded in the promise of eternal life. And, as also noted by Anglican theologian Andrew Shanks (2000), "Paul repeatedly invokes the presence of the God of *eirene* in situations of intra-community conflict that need resolving. One of the main immediate purposes of the epistles, in general, is to help maintain peace within the churches."

For the Church since the fourth-century, "peace" has been central to God's invitation to join one another in communion with Christ at the Eucharistic table. Not only does it embrace the wholeness of *shalom* and the salvation gained through Jesus' death and resurrection, it also empowers us to extend that unbounded joy to all whose lives we might touch. "The peace of the Lord be with you . . . and also with you" is, indeed, the greeting of faith met with our welcoming response.

What, then, might this "peace" mean for our embrace of new clergy? To be sure, a rector's first few months will be filled with "meet and greets," coffee conversations and lunches, and any number of other activities organized by the congregation to introduce themselves to her and the larger community. Although participating in this orientation, the vestry has several distinct responsibilities in extending the congregation's welcome.

First, it's obliged wherever possible to resolve contentious issues before the new rector's tenure begins to ensure that the baggage of the past does not encumber the opportunities for the future. In addition, it's critical that the lessons learned be shared with the rector early in her tenure to provide insight into the vestry's problem resolution process and the growth experienced as leaders and a governing body.

Likely, a new rector will be overwhelmed by demands on her time. Most will be well-intended overtures to establish a relationship, as well as to share details of the congregation's specific ministries and hopes for the future. On the other hand, some will seize the transition as an opportunity to pursue personal agendas, advocating for changes that previously had been rejected. The vestry has an important role in both circumstances—urging the congregation to give the rector the space to absorb a new organizational and social environment at a measured pace and providing context and perspective for proposals emanating from beyond the congregation's normal decision-making process.

New rectors bring change—some subtle and others dramatic. The vestry is challenged to prepare itself and the parish for it—not necessarily a specific change but rather for the means to embrace conversations about change and the discernment of its possibilities. Plowing the congregation's spiritual ground for planting the seeds of change is an important role for the vestry in welcoming a new rector's vision and aspirations.

The temptation to "get moving" will be palpable and enticing. Although the vestry should share in this sense of missional urgency with the rector, it also must restrain the urge to act too soon and too quickly. The work of the Church is a marathon, not a sprint.

Perhaps most important among its functions, the vestry is chartered to capture the joy of new leadership, share it with the congregation, make it known to the rector, and embody it in their work together. "The peace of the Lord be with you . . . and also with you." May joy reign!

Vestry Discussion

- As a vestry, how do we ensure that we don't allow congregational baggage to accumulate?
- How do we best prepare our congregation for the inevitable change that occurs with the transition of clergy?
- What can the vestry do to help ensure that new clergy are not inundated with requests (however well-intended) and have the time and space to acclimate to the congregation gradually?
- Are there specific activities that should be untaken by the vestry to build a relationship with new clergy?

Something to Ponder

Although hospitality and welcome are central to congregational life and its presence within the community, receiving a new rector requires careful and purposeful planning that reveals the Spirit at work among all the faithful. The Eucharistic exchange of the peace captures what we hope to achieve in a new relationship between the vestry and its spiritual leader. And since it involves multiple parties, you're invited to consider the concept of "mutuality" and your expectations of it when preparing for a clergy transition.

NURTURING THE SOUL

Where It All Began: Knitting Our "Ahas" Together

Opening Prayer

O God, whose Spirit discovers and invites us into the fullness of your being: touch our souls, warm our hearts, overcome our doubts, enliven our faith, and empower our ministry that we may truly know and serve you as disciples of the living Christ. Amen.

A Quote for Your Consideration

Each of us has a unique faith journey and narrative that describes it. To be sure, there are many points along the way that mark our spiritual trek and hold special meaning. The Church's rites of baptism and confirmation are certainly two of them. But for many of us, there also are those distinct and unscripted moments of epiphany—of an encounter with the Divine—that we recall as if they were truly the beginning of our faith. The nineteenth-century Anglican priest and founder of the Methodist movement John Wesley provides an especially moving description of just such an experience (Heitzenrater, 1995):

> In the evening I went very unwillingly to a society in Aldersgate Street, where one was reading Luther's

Preface to the Epistle to the Romans. About a quarter before nine, while he was describing the change which God works in the heart through faith in Christ, I felt my heart strangely warmed. I felt I did trust in Christ, Christ alone for salvation, and an assurance was given me that he had taken away *my* sins, even *mine*, and saved *me* from the law of sin and death.

These spiritual "Aha" moments are so essential to understanding the lives of individual parishioners, as well as the collective congregation, that vestries and clergy would serve them well by exploring ways in which their stories might be told and woven into the lifeblood of the church. Revisiting personal epiphanies—those special moments when faith came into clear focus—also provides congregational leaders with the space and context for spiritual renewal, especially in moments of doubt or despair.

Leadership in Context

Many of us have shared Wesley's unexpected, life-changing encounter with God. For some, it may have been Scripture or sacred music heard as never before. For others, it was the "still small voice" of God amid a personal crisis. And for yet some others, it was the Spirit's call to monastic life or ordained ministry. These "Aha" moments are as many and varied as the people who've experienced them. However, they share a profound sense of the Divine entering into an individual's daily life and forever changing it. And there's no more obvious example than Saul's conversion on the road to Damascus recounted in the Book of Acts (9.1–22):

Meanwhile Saul, still breathing threats and murder against the disciples of the Lord, went to the high priest and asked him for letters to the synagogues at Damascus, so that if he found any who belonged to the Way, men or women, he might bring them bound to Jerusalem. Now as he was going along and approaching Damascus, suddenly a light from heaven flashed around him. He fell to the ground and heard a voice saying to him, "Saul, Saul, why do you persecute me?" He asked, "Who are you, Lord?" The reply came, "I am Jesus, whom you are persecuting. But get up and enter the city, and you will be told what you are to do." The men who were traveling with him stood speechless because they heard the voice but saw no one. Saul got up from the ground, and though his eyes were open, he could see nothing; so they led him by the hand and brought him into Damascus. For three days he was without sight, and neither ate nor drank.

Now there was a disciple in Damascus named Ananias. The Lord said to him in a vision, "Ananias." He answered, "Here I am, Lord." The Lord said to him, "Get up and go to the street called Straight, and at the house of Judas look for a man of Tarsus named Saul. At this moment he is praying, and he has seen in a vision a man named Ananias come in and lay his hands on him so that he might regain his sight." But Ananias answered, "Lord, I have heard from many about this man, how much evil he has done to your saints in Jerusalem, and here he has authority from the chief priests to bind all who invoke your name." But the Lord said to him, "Go, for he is an instrument whom I have chosen to bring my name before Gentiles and kings and before the people of Israel; I myself will show him how much he must suffer for the sake of my name." So Ananias went and entered the house. He laid his hands on Saul and said, "Brother Saul, the Lord Jesus, who appeared to you on your way here, has sent me so that you may regain your sight and be filled with the Holy Spirit." And immediately something like scales fell from his eyes, and his sight was restored. Then he got up and was baptized, and after taking some food, he regained his strength. For several days he was with the disciples in Damascus, and immediately he began to proclaim Jesus in the synagogues, saying, "He is the Son of God." All who heard him were amazed and said, "Is not this the man who made havoc in Jerusalem among those who invoked this name? And has he not come here for the purpose of bringing them bound before the chief priests?" Saul became increasingly more powerful and confounded the Jews who lived in Damascus by proving that Jesus was the Messiah.

To be sure, few of us have been tossed to the ground or blinded by a light in our most intimate encounters with God. But also, few of us have been on a mission to capture Christians and bring them to court! Nevertheless, Saul's conversion narrative has much to offer as we reflect on our own experiences and those of our fellow travelers in faith.

Perhaps most obvious is that the encounter occurred as he was going about his daily routine. Amid simply doing his job (however despicable it was), God transformed an otherwise normal day into one that reoriented Saul's entire life and changed the world forever. Like Saul, our own "Aha" moments are particularly defining because they intervene when we least expect them. They catch us off guard and unable to throw up a defense. We're simply enveloped in that instant and transported to a dimension of the Divine we've not previously experienced.

So too do these personal epiphanies change the trajectory of our lives. While they occur at a specific moment in time, they continue to shape our faith journeys. A few years ago, for example, I had the privilege of participating in a seminar on the life and poetry of John Donne led by the Very Rev. John Moses, KCVO, the retired Dean of St. Paul's Cathedral in London. Over tea one afternoon, I shared that my journey from Lutheranism to the Episcopal Church began with chance attendance at Evensong at St. Paul's years before. He leaned back in his chair and smiled proudly, noting the many people during his tenure who had a similar experience. We spent the rest of our conversation discussing how that single moment renewed a faith that had waned and set me on the path toward the priesthood—hardly what I had anticipated the second act of my career would be!

Finally (but admittedly speculatively), it seems reasonable to assume that Paul (nee Saul) regularly revisited and reflected on that incredible encounter on the Damascus Road, drawing strength from it especially in the most dire of circumstances. Similarly, John Wesley did in recalling his Aldersgate experience, and I can attest to the continuing significance of Evensong at St. Paul's in my life and ministry.

Faith communities are extraordinarily complex social systems that reflect a variety of individual experiences and perspectives knit together to shape the congregation's ethos. Although the system itself often acquires a life of its own, the individual stories of its members are central to understanding a congregation and leading its spiritual growth. Among the most powerful are those unexpected moments when God breaks into people's lives, transforms them, and reorients their faith journeys. The challenge for congregational leaders is to facilitate the integration of these narratives into the church's story and to summon them—individually and collectively—to strengthen and embolden the saints for ministry.

Vestry Discussion

- Can you recall an "Aha" moment in your life with God, and how has it shaped your faith journey?
- Do you revisit this experience and, if so, how does it function in your spiritual life and relationships with others?
- Has your experience provided specific insight into your role as a member of the vestry and congregational leader?
- How might your "Aha" experience and those of the parish be shared and used to shape the congregation's ministries?

Something to Ponder

Regardless of how extraordinary or profound, I suspect each of us has been gobsmacked by the Spirit at some point in our lives, perhaps even several times. You're invited to consider the impact of an "Aha" moment on your faith journey and how it might be shared to facilitate the vestry's spiritual formation, as well as the congregation's.

Making Disciples: Bringing Christ to the World

Opening Prayer

Most gracious and loving God who in every moment of our lives summons us to discipleship: strengthen our faith and deepen our understanding of you; grant us courage to bear witness to the Good News in Christ Jesus to all whose lives we touch; give us joy as we engage in this journey; and make your Spirit known to those who hunger for your life-giving presence. In the name of your Son, we pray. Amen.

A Quote for Your Consideration

Amid the changing contours of American culture, differences in generational needs and expectations and penetrating questions about the role religion can play in forming community, churches continue to struggle with issues of sustainability and growth. Programs are created, liturgies updated, and preaching made more relevant to the lived experience of those who gather for worship. The hope is that they will help retain current members and attract new ones, with significant time spent by clergy and vestries fine-tuning these initiatives and attaching labels like *outreach*, *renewal*, and *engagement* to them. Despite their well-intended objectives, they nonetheless reflect a particularly institutionalized response to the challenges of congregational development. Too often lacking, however, is "equipping the saints for discipleship," preparing every member of the parish to proclaim the Good News of the Gospel in their own distinctive way in their daily lives. It's in fact this work—evangelism—to which Jesus has called us, ministry fundamental to our very being as the Body of Christ, an imperative put forward by Episcopal priest and psychologist David Gortner (2008):

> Evangelism is your natural expression of gratitude for God's goodness. Gratitude and wonder, born of grace, drive evangelism, propelling you outward beyond yourself to places you have not gone before. Your story compels you to give to others, expressing in word and deed the wonder and delight of God's love for you and all humanity ... Evangelism is not something one simply does to another for another's sake, but it is a spiritual discipline that nurtures and transforms the one who bears good news and recognizes God at work in others.

Leadership in Context

Episcopalians are not alone in our aversion to evangelism. For most mainline Protestants and Roman Catholics, the

"E-word" conjures up images of aggressive Bible thumpers in the public square, church folks trying to push their way through our front doors for a conversion moment and the ubiquitous presence of two young men purposefully strolling through our neighborhoods hoping to engage people in discussions of faith. Rooted in the Great Commission to "Go therefore and make disciples of all nations..." (Matthew 28.19a), these heartfelt, genuine expressions of discipleship have undoubtedly succeeded in welcoming many to faith. Likewise, the international missionary societies established by many denominations in the nineteenth century were propelled by the desire for global outreach. Certainly, these efforts reflect a dimension of evangelism but arguably do not define it. Nor do they feature prominently in most of our lives.

As Gortner (2008) reminds us, evangelism in its essence is a personal response to God's unbounded grace, not an institutional program. And at the heart of its message is the reality of Jesus' life and ministry (Luke 4.18–19):

> The Spirit of the Lord is upon me [Jesus],
>   because he has anointed me
>   to bring good news to the poor.
> He has sent me to proclaim release to
>   the captives
>   and recovery of sight to the blind,
>   to set free those who are oppressed,
> to proclaim the year of the Lord's favor.

Or as former Episcopal Presiding Bishop the Rt. Rev. Michael Curry has often remarked, "If it's not about love, it's not about

God." Therefore, if the foundation of evangelism is in the shared experience and conversations of individuals grounded in the mercy and compassion of a loving God, what additionally might we understand and apply to the ministry to which each of us has been called?

Accepting evangelism as a spiritual discipline deeply rooted in reflection, prayer, and thoughtful engagement is the bedrock of discipleship. It's a process that invites us to consider the Divine grace we've experienced, the ways in which we might bear witness to it, and the opportunities for both intentional and serendipitous interaction with the broader community. The discipline also summons us to prayer—for insight, clarity, and courage as we prepare to activate the discipleship to which we've been called. Opening ourselves to sharing the Gospel that has formed our faith in the varied circumstances of our lives is the fulfillment of Jesus' summons to make the Good News known to all.

Although evangelism is not fundamentally an institutional program, it nonetheless requires congregational and denominational support. Let's face it, bearing public witness to our faith is a challenge for most of us. We don't want to offend. We don't want to be vulnerable. We don't know what to say or do. Thankfully, the familiar quote often attributed to St. Francis of Assisi, "Preach the Gospel at all times, and when necessary, use words," offers much needed encouragement. Foundational to evangelism is reflecting Christ in the way we interact with each other and the world, the basic actions of Christian discipleship. However, the ability and desire to share the source of our faith with authenticity and ease is often learned behavior—modeled for us by others and taught in both structured courses and informal discussions. Creating an environment that invites parishioners to explore evangelism and equip them with the skills to communicate effectively is an important role for congregational leaders, as well as their regional and national partners.

Equally important is the recognition that evangelism is not an event or even an encounter, but rather an ongoing journey for both the disciple and those to whom the witness of faith is borne. Listening intentionally to one another, ensuring time and space to process information and emotions, and respecting the integrity and individuality of the exchange are essential. While this may not come naturally for many of us (especially in the context of evangelism), vestries with the assistance of independent consultants and denominational resources can structure opportunities to enhance the critical listening and information processing skills of the parishioners they serve.

Finally, we need to be clear about the focus of evangelism. The goal is not to fill our pews. It's not to increase pledges or plate offerings. And it's not even to expand the congregation's capacity for community outreach. Rather as David Gortner (2008) wisely concludes, evangelism is "not of and for the church, but of and for the Holy Spirit," a perspective beautifully captured in the Episcopal Hymn #512 (1982), "Come, Gracious Spirit, Heavenly Dove":

> Come, gracious Spirit, heavenly dove
> with light and comfort from above;
> be thou our guardian, thou our guide,
> o'er every thought and step preside.

The light of truth to us display,
and make us know and choose the way;
plant holy fear in every heart,
that we from thee may ne'er depart.

Lead us to Christ, the living way,
nor let us from his precepts stray;
lead us to holiness, the road
that we must take to dwell with God.

Lead us to heaven, that we may share
fullness of joy for ever there;
lead us to God, our final rest,
to be with him for ever blest.

Vestry Discussion

- How does "evangelism" resonate in your personal life, as well as in your vestry leadership?
- What do you need to be prepared "to make disciples"?
- What experience (if any) has your congregation had with organized evangelism training and initiatives? What were the results?
- How might your vestry and clergy instill a greater spirit of evangelism in your congregation?

Something to Ponder

Among the most well-known quotations from Scripture is Matthew's recounting of the Great Commission to go throughout the world making disciples of Christ. This concept has been interpreted in different ways, from local initiatives to international programs. In the context of Jesus' witness to us, you're encouraged to consider the meaning of *commission* in your life and the practice of your faith.

Faith Seeking Understanding

Opening Prayer

God of all wisdom and knowledge, who excites our imagination, nurtures our faith, and nourishes our search for truth: bless our curiosity; guide our study and reflection; and lead us into a fuller and more intimate relationship with you and all your creation. We humbly pray in Jesus' Name. Amen.

A Quote for Your Consideration

Most vestry members accept this ministry out of a profound sense of service, sharing their distinct experiences, skills, and perspectives in the leadership of their faith communities. (Alright, from time to time there's some clerical arm twisting!) Nominating committees regularly recruit individuals with financial acumen, legal backgrounds, and management and consulting expertise, among several skill sets. Seldom, however, does the role of professional educator—particularly one with a theological bent—surface as a criterion for vestry nomination. Although no doubt valuing the role of education in the ongoing process of Christian formation, it frequently is assumed that clergy and staff will fulfill this role for both the vestry and the congregation. However, nineteenth-century theologian and founder of the Christian Socialist movement Frederick Denison Maurice cautions us against an inordinate reliance on "private judgement" and, by implication, urges congregational leaders—clergy and laity alike—to advance theological education within their parishes (2002b):

> This age is impatient of distinctions—of the distinction between right and wrong, as well as that between truth and falsehood. Of all its perils, this seems to me the greatest . . . I should always denounce the glorification of private judgment, as fatal to the belief in truth, and to the pursuit of it. We are always tending towards the notion that we may think what we like to think; that there is no standard to which our thoughts should be conformed . . . But dogmatism is not the antagonist of private judgment. The most violent assertor of his private judgment is the greatest dogmatist. And, conversely, the loudest assertor of the dogmatic authority of the church, is very apt to be the most vehement and fanatical stickler for his own private judgements.

Leadership in Context

For many of us, our theological education is largely limited to those minutes in the pew on Sunday morning listening to a preacher expound on Scripture, frame the message in the context of the great dogmas of the Church, and hopefully apply them to the challenges of our daily lives. Sadly, most of us are not regular participants in structured Bible study, book clubs with a religious focus, or theological group discussions of the issues of the day. Even if we routinely engage in private study and reflection, we miss the opportunity for spiritual growth that flourishes in the exchange of ideas and perspectives with others. And consequently, we leave ourselves vulnerable to the hubris Maurice denounces, "the glorification of private judgment."

The collective wisdom of the Church—from the synods of early Christendom to the denominational conventions of today—has long been the corrective to the extremes of individual interpretation, flawed scholarship, and heretical doctrine (at least over time). Historically, these pivotal moments have been grounded not only in vigorous debate but also in deep study and prayer, perhaps best characterized by the eleventh-century Benedictine monk St. Anselm of Canterbury, who thoughtfully observed that theology is "faith seeking understanding."

Individual faith communities certainly benefit from the shared experience and insights of the Church worldwide. But additionally, they have the potential to ferment vigorous theological debate and transformation locally. Critical, however, is access to the resources that enrich the discussion and provide a common vocabulary for it. Toward that end, a parish library can be an especially important and accessible source for both. And the size of the collection truly doesn't matter. Rather, the distribution of books and monographs across the broad spectrum of theology, their varied levels of scholarly sophistication, and the appeal to people at various junctures of their faith journey are the central elements to a library that fully serves the needs of an entire congregation.

Yet, Maurice's concern is not mitigated solely by access to materials that might expand our theological horizons. Essential is the communal opportunity to explore new dimensions of faith, to share our perspectives, and to learn from companions on faith's often bumpy road. More than merely providing financial support for books and other theological resources, vestries and parish faith leaders must assert the importance of Christian education and formation, establish organizational priorities that reflect this commitment, and provide the direction and funding to achieve these objectives.

The knowledge and wisdom gained from shared theological inquiry, reflection, and debate are essential to the life of a parish, its spiritual health, and its capacity for ministry. In his Letter to the Colossians (1.9–10), St. Paul punctuated just this point:

> For this reason, since the day we heard it, we have not ceased praying for you and asking that you may be filled with the knowledge of God's will in all spiritual wisdom and understanding, so that you may lead lives worthy of the Lord, fully pleasing to him, as you bear fruit in every good work and as you grow in the knowledge of God.

Certainly, the faith formation described by Paul is an ongoing process that not only enriches our spiritual and temporal lives but also girds us for work in a world so much in need of

God's grace and the Good News of the Gospel. Toward that end, vestries need to ensure ready access to the resources and venues that foster spiritual exploration and growth within the congregation and larger community, as well as opportunities to reveal new understanding amid the lived experience of faith.

Vestry Discussion

- To what extent is theological study part of your spiritual discipline? If it is, how has it shaped your faith and ministry?
- How might the vestry encourage theological education and reflection within the congregation?

Something to Ponder

In response to this essay, you're invited to reflect on "faith seeking understanding." However, rather than just ruminating on this phrase, challenge yourself to check out a book from your parish or public library on some aspect of theology of interest to you, read and consider its relevance to your faith journey and the congregation's, and then create an opportunity at an upcoming vestry meeting to share your thoughts. Hopefully, this will lead to a broader discussion of potential strategies to enhance theological education both in your congregation and the community at large.

Abundance in the Face of Scarcity

Opening Prayer

God of bounty beyond what we deserve or can comprehend: give us faith to confront the fear of scarcity that so dominates our personal and public discourse; give us hope as we enter the abundance of your grace; give us all that we need to care for the lives we might touch; and give us the wisdom to use your gifts to the glory of your Son, Jesus Christ. Amen.

A Quote for Your Consideration

We live in a world where scarcity is a dominant narrative ... and for understandable reasons. Climate changes have decimated agriculture across the globe. And war has left millions without adequate shelter, potable water, and security for displaced families. Although too often labeled "third-world problems," the reality is that developed countries also confront presumed scarcity and the politics surrounding it: food deserts in economically depressed neighborhoods; wide disparities in access to essential health-care services, and decaying infrastructure.

Certainly, these are complex socioeconomic, cultural, and political challenges. And as such, to even begin to resolve them requires innovative research, planning, and policy implementation. Similarly, churches regularly face the daunting task of resource allocation in which the need for services far outstrips what appears to be the available human and financial capital to address them. While we too frequently default to the arguments of scarcity, Episcopal priest and theologian Rev.

Dr. Ralph McMichael (2019) reminds us of the unfettered abundance of God's economy made present in the Eucharist.

> The faithful act of offering, or offering as the faithful act, is the fulcrum point of the Eucharistic economy. It is the definitive turning away from the "turn to subject" towards the turn to God. After this act of offering, all that we are, have been and will be belong to God. And we cannot look back to the more familiar and assuring confines of our own subjectivity. We have given up being the narrator of our own lives. For this offering to be proportional to the offering that we receive from God, it will be a total offering. An appropriate "offertory sentence" for the Eucharist could be, "into your hands I commend my spirit." Faith is baptismal and Eucharistic; it is being buried into the paschal mystery so that this mystery is the life we are raised into, and we offer our selves without remainder so that we would receive the gift of life from God. Nothing is held back; the gift is abundant life.

Leadership in Context

McMichael's students (and I was one) are fond of taking aim at his seemingly singular focus, affectionately joking that every theological question he poses has the same answer: "the Eucharist!" While good-natured fodder for classroom banter, the heckling underscores the truth of his argument. The Eucharist is at the very core of the Christian experience. It's that singular act that unites us with the fullness of God. It's the act that memorializes the infinite abundance of

God's grace made known in his Son's death and resurrection. And it's the Eucharist that summons us to share that same unlimited abundance with the entire world. Unquestionably, it's this liturgical act and all that it embodies that must be the foundation for any discussion of the way in which churches approach the support and funding of the ministries to which they've been called. It truly is the basis for our understanding of abundance even in the face of apparent scarcity.

The concept of God's unbridled abundance is not simply a tenet of faith. In fact, it's repeatedly revealed throughout Scripture, beginning with the creation narrative itself (Genesis 1.29–30):

> God said, "See, I have given you every plant yielding seed that is upon the face of all the earth, and every tree with seed in its fruit; you shall have them for food. And to every beast of the earth, and to every bird of the air, and to everything that creeps on the earth, everything that has the breath of life, I have given every green plant for food." And it was so.

The creation of everything that could ever be needed or desired defines the limitless abundance of God's gifts and grace made available to all from the very first moment of time. However, despite the richness of creation, doubt often undermined the faith of God's people, even amid their dramatic rescue from slavery in Egypt (Exodus 16.2–8):

> The whole congregation of the Israelites complained against Moses and Aaron in the wilderness. The Israelites said to them, "If only we had died by the

hand of the Lord in the land of Egypt, when we sat by the fleshpots and ate our fill of bread; for you have brought us out into this wilderness to kill this whole assembly with hunger." Then the Lord said to Moses, "I am going to rain bread from heaven for you, and each day the people shall go out and gather enough for that day. In that way I will test them, whether they will follow my instruction or not. On the sixth day, when they prepare what they bring in, it will be twice as much as they gather on other days." So Moses and Aaron said to all the Israelites, "In the evening you shall know that it was the Lord who brought you out of the land of Egypt, and in the morning you shall see the glory of the Lord, because he has heard your complaining against the Lord. For what are we, that you complain against us?" And Moses said, "When the Lord gives you meat to eat in the evening and your fill of bread in the morning, because the Lord has heard the complaining that you utter against him—what are we? Your complaining is not against us but against the Lord."

Nor were Jesus' own disciples immune from doubt, raising the issue of scarcity when confronted with the need to feed 5,000 hungry followers at the end of a long day of preaching in the Galilean town of Bethsaida (Luke 9.12–17):

The day was drawing to a close, and the twelve came to him and said, "Send the crowd away, so that they may go into the surrounding villages and countryside,

> to lodge and get provisions; for we are here in a deserted place." But he said to them, "You give them something to eat." They said, "We have no more than five loaves and two fish—unless we are to go and buy food for all these people." For there were about five thousand men. And he said to his disciples, "Make them sit down in groups of about fifty each." They did so and made them all sit down. And taking the five loaves and the two fish, he looked up to heaven and blessed and broke them and gave them to the disciples to set before the crowd. And all ate and were filled. What was left over was gathered up, twelve baskets of broken pieces.

Alas, you'd think that after centuries of being summoned to trust in a God who provides all that we could ever need or want, we'd get the message. Yet as if anticipating that we might again falter, we're given the eternal Presence as a reminder of the fullest expression of God's abundance—the gift of God's own Son made known in the Eucharist (Luke 22.19–20):

> Then he took a loaf of bread, and when he had given thanks he broke it and gave it to them, saying, "This is my body, which is given for you. Do this in remembrance of me." And he did the same with the cup after supper, saying, "This cup that is poured out for you is the new covenant in my blood."

The needs of churches and all they serve are many—so much so that they all too frequently overwhelm us and what we believe we can provide. In the Eucharist, however, we're reminded that faith and discipleship are grounded in God's economy of abundance, limited only by our imaginations and the priorities we embrace. This is neither pollyannish nor naïve.

I'm reminded, for example, of a parish that was struggling to increase its operating budget from $1 million to the $1.3 million needed to underwrite the breadth of its current ministries. The conversation among congregational leaders frequently was laced with the language of scarcity: "major contributors were dying or moving away; young people don't have the financial resources for sacrificial giving; and there's too much competition from other charities with which members are involved." There were serious questions about whether this enhanced level of giving could be achieved, let alone the $3 million annually that would allow the congregation to grow and sustain its pivotal presence in the community. Recently, this parish was confronted with the immediate need to assist clergy with housing and, in response to a direct appeal, raised more than the $300,000 requested in a matter of only several months. To be sure, funding special projects or programs is different than the annual appeal for operating capital. But the point is that the $300,000 the parish had been trying to find for several years was there all the time. The contributions came in various amounts from across the broad spectrum of the congregation. Whether these one-time gifts can be converted to annual pledges remains to be determined. What is clear, however, is the opportunity to change the narrative from one of scarcity to that of abundance—to live into the Eucharist.

As reflected in this brief vignette, the challenge for vestries, clergy, and the congregations they serve is to embrace God's abundance in the Eucharist as foundational for worship, spiritual growth, strategic planning, policy development, and resource allocation. It's the challenge to reimagine the structure and support of the work we're called to do. It's the challenge to set our individual and congregational priorities with the certainty of God's abundance. And it's the challenge of faith—to believe that God indeed will provide all that we need. As Ralph McMichael noted, the Eucharist is not only the answer to our yearning but also the beginning of faithful discipleship in the name of the risen Christ.

Vestry Discussion

- How do you understand the meaning of living a Eucharistic faith?
- How does the Eucharist's celebration of God's unfettered abundance impact your piety, as well as personal decisions and those you consider as a member of the vestry?
- How might a focus on God's abundance change your congregational life?
- What do you as congregational leaders need to do to facilitate this transformation?

Something to Ponder

At the heart of the Eucharistic is Christ's charge to celebrate "in remembrance of me." You're invited to consider the impact of this sacrament on your personal faith journey, your vestry ministry and how it might shape the congregation's discipleship.

Catch Your Breath . . .
But Hold on to Your Seat

Opening Prayer

Lord God, who calms the troubled waters that swirl around our lives: grant us respite from the bustle, worries, and challenges of the day; clear the fog that clouds our vision and diminishes our ministry; prepare us for the unexpected; and gift us with the Spirit of unbounded hope and joyful anticipation. All this we pray in Jesus' Name. Amen.

A Quote for Your Consideration

Leadership is demanding. It's tough. And it's exhausting. Whether serving on the board of a multinational corporation or a local church vestry, governance can be a slog. The issues are often complex, the solutions elusive, and the outcomes unpredictable. So, there's little wonder that management consultants, governance gurus, and spiritual directors are united in their recommendation periodically to call "time out" to recover and regenerate. The following quote from eighteenth-century Anglican priest and founder of the Methodist movement John Wesley (2002) punctuates the importance of this dimension of self-care:

> Men are generally lost in the hurry of life, in the business or pleasures of it, and seem to think that their regeneration, their new nature, will spring and grow up within them, with as little care and thought of their own as their bodies were conceived and have

attained their full strength and stature; whereas, there is nothing more certain than that the Holy Spirit will not purify our nature, unless we carefully attend to his motions.

Leadership in Context

The need for regular rest—sabbath—is essential for a healthy life, productive work, and stable relationships. From the very beginning of creation, even God recognized that periodically stepping away from daily routines provides the opportunity for reflection and recovery:

> And on the sixth day God finished the work he had done, and he rested on the seventh day from all the work that he had done. So God blessed the seventh day and hallowed it, because on it God rested from all the work that he had done in creation (Genesis 2.2–3).

Both the academic and popular literature—secular as well as religious—are replete with accounts of the benefits of time for individual rest, recovery, and renewal. Less explored, however, is the need for the collective sabbath of leadership teams, including vestries. To be sure, the practice of organizational retreats is longstanding in both the corporate and ecclesiastical world. Although the agenda of these sessions often includes time to decompress, reflect, and prepare for future challenges, the focus typically is on operational reviews, strategic planning, and goal setting. Unfortunately, structuring the activities, interactions, and time necessary for the team collectively to "catch its breath" is too often overlooked and sacrificed for more tangible outcomes. And the consequences for the leadership team as well as its individual members can be significant, including deterioration of the group's cohesion, becoming overwhelmed by current circumstances, and, perhaps most important, the inability to prepare for the unexpected. Alternatively, the experience of Jesus' disciples following the feeding of the 5,000 (Matthew 14.22–33) dramatically models the critical importance of collective sabbath time for executive teams, governing bodies and vestries:

> Immediately he made the disciples get into the boat and go on ahead to the other side, while he dismissed the crowds. And after he had dismissed the crowds, he went up the mountain by himself to pray. When evening came, he was there alone, but by this time the boat, battered by the waves, was far from the land, for the wind was against them. And early in the morning he came walking toward them on the sea. But when the disciples saw him walking on the sea, they were terrified, saying, "It is a ghost!" And they cried out in fear. But immediately Jesus spoke to them and said, "Take heart, it is I; do not be afraid." Peter answered him, "Lord, if it is you, command me to come to you on the water." He said, "Come." So Peter got out of the boat, started walking on the water, and came toward Jesus. But when he noticed the strong wind, he became frightened, and beginning to sink, he cried out, "Lord, save me!" Jesus immediately reached out his hand and caught him, saying to him, "You of little faith, why did you doubt?" When they got into the boat, the wind

ceased. And those in the boat worshiped him, saying, "Truly you are the Son of God."

The mass picnic served up by Jesus and his disciples was both a miracle and a logistical nightmare—so much so that he felt the need to gather himself privately in prayer afterward and dispatched his erstwhile followers to a boat on the Sea of Galilee for their own respite from the crowds and the frenzy of the moment. Instinctively, Jesus understood the need for time away from the physical and emotional demands of the active ministry in which he and his disciples were engaged—time to reflect, recover, and re-energize. Things seem to have gone well for Jesus but not so much for the twelve. Unexpectedly, they found themselves battling a tempest and encountering what they imagined to be an apparition. Only when Jesus returned to them, rescued Peter, and calmed the turbulent waters was this surprising situation resolved.

There's much to be gleaned from this familiar story. It illustrates the need for individual as well as collective recovery from intense emotional, physical, and spiritual experiences. Although the context for Jesus and the disciples was different—a retreat to personal prayer versus what was hoped to be a quiet time floating on the water—both offered a setting to respectively "catch their breath." Too frequently overlooked, however, is the importance of using sabbath time to prepare for the unexpected, not knowing what or when it will occur but with the certainty that something will come up that challenges us when we least expect it. The disciples learned this hard lesson relaxing in the boat only soon to be buffeted by rough seas.

Vestries regularly find themselves engaged in particularly demanding situations—the recruitment of a new rector, leadership of a major capital campaign, and the reconfiguration of worship space, to name only a few. Just as planning retreats were critical to the launch of these initiatives, so too is structured time to step back from the intensity of the work, reflect on the experience, explore the lessons learned, and, especially important, prepare for the next unanticipated challenge or crisis. Essential is that this be both an individual and collective effort. The structure of these sabbaths will vary significantly depending on the specific issue, the challenges it posed, and the interaction of the leadership group in addressing it. At the very least, we would do well to embrace the words of the traditional spiritual, "Steal away, steal away with Jesus."

Vestry Discussion

- Do you regularly allot time for sabbath? If so, how do you practice it, and what are the elements that distinguish it from your daily routine?
- What in your spiritual life most cries out for refreshment and renewal?
- Can you recall a specific sabbath experience that was especially memorable in the insight you gained into your relationship with God?

Something to Ponder

Each of us regularly needs to pause and reflect on various aspects of our lives as Christ's disciples and explore ways to revive and enrich our faith. How do you individually and the vestry collectively seek opportunities for "renewal"?

Be Still

Opening Prayer

Most welcoming God, who knits us together as a community and draws us into conversation with you and one another: open us to the movement of your Spirit as we listen to the hopes and aspirations of your faithful; keep us mindful of the truth of our congregation as we imagine our future; and grant us the courage to hear your voice. All for the love of your Son. Amen.

A Quote for Your Consideration

Although "discernment" has gradually crept into the language of corporations and popular culture in the past several decades, it remains most closely associated with the spiritual practices of religious traditions—Christian, Jewish, Muslim, and others. Whether in the consideration of a new direction for a congregation, the allocation of its resources, or an individual's call to an ordained life, discernment is a distinct process that can and must be inculcated and nurtured in the work of vestries. Toward that end, the twentieth-century Trappist monk, theologian, and social activist Thomas Merton offers wise counsel in a prayer adapted from his work, *Thoughts in Solitude* (Farnham et al. 1991):

God, we have no idea where we are going. We do not see the road ahead of us. We cannot know for certain where it will end. Nor do we really know ourselves, and the fact that we think we are following your will does not mean that we are actually doing so. But we believe that the desire to please you does in fact please you. And we hope we have that desire in all that we are doing. We hope we will never do anything apart from that desire. And we know that if we do this you will lead us by the right road, though we may know nothing about it. Therefore, we will trust you always though we may seem to be lost and in the shadow of death. We will not fear, for you are ever with us, and you will never leave us to face our perils alone.

Leadership in Context

For clergy, as well as many lay people, the notion of discernment conjures up the process of assisting an individual in determining a call to ordained ministry. The journey is spiritually and emotionally rigorous and lengthy, and it engages both the depth of personal reflection and the breadth of the Church's interests. Although a quite specific context for spiritual discernment, it certainly is not the sole circumstance in which this process can and should occur or its methods be employed. In fact, for the faithful individually and communally, discernment—determining what spirit (God's or another's) is at work in a decision-making process—is an essential component of the life to which we're called, a point made abundantly clear in the First Letter of John (4.1): "Beloved, do not believe every spirit, but test the spirits to see whether they are from God." In the ethos of discernment, spirits are not the ugly creatures that inhabit dark places but rather are to be understood as the forces that shape us (for good or ill) in a particular moment—humility, love, greed, and selfishness, for example, not to mention the Spirit of God made present in the Good News of Jesus Christ. The challenge, therefore, for vestries and their decision-making processes, is to explore the question, "What would God have us do?" and answer it in the context of the Gospel. Mark McIntosh's especially thoughtful study, *Discernment and Truth: The Spirituality and Theology of Knowledge* (2004), offers important guidance on the conditions necessary for the process to succeed regardless of the issue being considered.

Central to the work of vestry discernment, he argues, is trust in the Spirit of God moving and working among us. Ours is not a God who plays "stump the faithful," gaming us as we search for the truth in a specific situation. Rather, this Spirit opens us to possibilities previously unseen, relationships not imagined, and directions unexplored. At its core, however, the legitimacy of any claim to be God's truth ultimately is validated solely by its reflection of the unbridled love and unbounded mercy of the Gospel made manifest in the life, death, and resurrection of Jesus Christ. It is this trust that the process of spiritual discernment will reveal the will of God that gives all of us, including vestries, hope.

Trust also is demanded of each other in our search for the Spirit of God. An open heart and mind, as well as transparency, selflessness, and honesty, are critical to ensuring the integrity of the process and the decisions that result.

Second, McIntosh notes that Christian discernment attempts to differentiate the Spirit of God from other forces at work in our lives. To be sure, there are many spirits that enrich us—the spirit of teamwork, for example, and the spirit of holidays shared with family and friends. So too, however, are we daily confronted by the forces of evil that cloud our vision of God and undermine our pursuit of the Divine in the decisions that challenge us. Determining what is shaping our deliberations in a particular circumstance is a task that requires our willingness to confront both good and evil. On the one hand, the spirit of evil is evidenced in anger, turmoil, jealousy, revulsion, and resistance. Alternatively, good is marked by love, joy, hope, and a sense of profound harmony with the world we share. Prayer, listening, and quiet conversation are attributes that will serve vestries particularly well in discerning the path forward for the congregations they serve.

No doubt, the very concept of spiritual discernment strikes many of us as an elusive mystery far beyond our grasp. Although not a utilitarian quest for what is best for the most people or the straightforward application of sensible values and moral codes, Christian discernment is, in fact, the search for practical wisdom (McIntosh 2004). It's the process of problem-solving through which we mine the depths of God in Scripture and the ecclesiastical traditions we've inherited using our capacity to reason. The result allows us not just to conceptualize a complex issue but to resolve it in a way that captures the truth of God.

Yet, Pilate poses a question for the ages in his interrogation of Jesus. "What is truth?" (John 18.38). In the context of Christian discernment, truth emerges not as an esoteric claim but rather as that which magnifies the majesty of God. Again, McIntosh (2004) offers a succinct description of this search for truth, noting that the "discernment of the truth of God's will always seeks to serve the greater *glory* of God, so that the radiance of the divine beauty and goodness can become manifest in the world...This discernment of the true divine intention in all things seeks to make that truth more visible, more luminous, as the beauty of holiness." Therefore, in addressing the many challenges that confront vestries, we're summoned to evaluate possibilities and render decisions that glorify God and fully reflect the Divine Presence.

Finally, discernment is best pursued and fulfilled when it's integral to a vestry's ongoing search for wisdom and flows from the congregation's vision, mission, and values. It's not merely a tool to facilitate decision-making within a community of faith; it's a consistent way of being and working. It's also grounded in patience even in the face of the most urgent questions.

May your vestry leadership always be grounded in patience and trust, the search for wisdom, and the goodness and truth of God. And may it be bolstered by the prayerful hope shared by English poet and parson George Herbert and quoted in Richard Harries' *Wounded I Sing: From Advent to Christmas with George Herbert* (2024):

> For my heart's desire
> Unto thine is bent:
>   I aspire
> To a full consent.

Not a word or look
I affect to own,
  But by book,
And thy book alone.

Vestry Discussion

- Has your vestry been trained in the process of discernment? If so, how has it facilitated decision-making? If not, would it help?
- How does the process of Christian discernment integrate with or complement other models of organizational decision-making?
- Is there something in your vestry's customary decision-making process that could be improved? If so, what?
- How might the process of discernment be extended to all in your parish who might want to explore potentially significant life decisions in the context and with the support of their faith community?

Something to Ponder

The specific framework we use for vestry decision-making, as well as the process through which it's accomplished, speak to the heart of our individual and collective spirituality. The results are expected to glorify God and reflect practical wisdom and Divine truth. Consequently, you're invited to consider the meaning and application of "truth" in the work of your vestry.

On Bended Knee

Opening Prayer

Almighty God, who invites our petitions and thanksgivings: salve our wounded souls; hear our cries for justice and peace; calm our restlessness and doubt; lift our voices in praise; and grant us the hope and certain knowledge of the Resurrection and eternal life. In Jesus' Name, we pray. Amen.

A Quote for Your Consideration

We Episcopalians perhaps most clearly distinguish ourselves from other expressions of the Christian faith by the relative absence of formalized dogma. Although our tradition abounds with poets, philosophers, and social activists, we're not known for our systematic theologians—let alone for doctrinal tomes, ecclesiastical encyclicals, and extensive dictates on the behavior expected of us. Certainly, we ascribe to the Catechism and other historical documents included in The Book of Common Prayer (1979). The hymns we regularly sing in worship also offer lyrical insight into the depth and breadth of our understanding of God's many facets. And we treasure centuries of topical scholarship proffered by clergy and laypersons alike.

But foremost, we pray what we believe (a loose translation of *lex orandi, lex credendi*). Rather than an almost infinite collection of theological perspectives authored and scattered across millennia, the Anglican tradition has instead integrated its beliefs into the structured form of prayers used for both collective and individual worship—The Book of Common

Prayer (1979). Indeed, many of us have found great comfort in the knowledge that millions around the globe are offering up the same faith shared in the same prayers.

At a time of considerable social and civic unrest, international crises, and the challenges of a planet in flux, it seems especially appropriate that we consider the essence of prayer, the many ways in which it's offered, and the impact it has on our lives and relationship with God. The observation of nineteenth-century Anglican evangelical and social activist Hannah More provides a crisp response (2002):

> Prayer is the application of want to him who alone can relieve it, the voice of sin to whom alone can pardon it. It is the urgency of poverty, the prostration of humility, the fervency of penitence, the confidence of trust. It is not eloquence, but earnestness; not figures of speech, but compunction of soul.

Leadership in Context

In many respects, the nature and context of prayer are elusive. Prayers reflect our virtually limitless requests and thanksgivings and are offered in every imaginable setting—from foxholes to sanctuaries, subways to hospital rooms, and lakeshores to mountain tops. This incredible diversity reminds me of an exchange during a bishop's visitation several years ago. The bishop had been reflecting on the importance of spiritual discipline and prayer during the adult formation time and coffee hour between Sunday services. A beloved but especially feisty parishioner challenged him, stating that her best moments of prayer were in the car driving to work each morning. He listened intently and nodded, seeming to understand and maybe even approve. But then the bishop leaned forward, shared just the hint of a smile, and responded that the convenience of drive time was attractive and not to be diminished, but that, "It's even more important to spend time on our knees, humbling ourselves in the presence of an Almighty God." Touché!

With such an exceptional range of possibilities, how might we more fully understand prayer as fundamental to our own spirituality, as well as in the life of the parish we serve and lead? Prayer in the Christian tradition begins with the psalms of ancient Israel recited individually and in corporate worship. The topics reflect the personal and national circumstances of God's people and include psalms of lament, praise, thanksgiving, trust, wisdom, and royal kingship and covenant. Not surprisingly, these psalms were appropriated by the nascent Jewish-Christian community and integrated into the evolving shape of its liturgy.

In addition to the psalms he prayed, Jesus' very life provides the cornerstone for both the shape and substance of Christian prayer, noted by the Anglican theologian Charles Miller, who asserts that "Jesus *is* the perfect prayer" (1995). His life, death, and resurrection are nothing less than a continuous, personal conversation with God, most clearly reflected in the words shared with Jesus' disciples at their last meal together:

> While they were eating, Jesus took a loaf of bread, and after blessing it he broke it, gave it to the disciples, and said, "Take, eat; this is my body." Then he took a cup, and after giving thanks he gave it to them,

saying, "Drink from it, all of you; for this is my blood of the covenant, which is poured out for many for the forgiveness of sins" (Matthew 26.26–28).

Over the next several centuries, this simple expression of thanksgiving expanded and became institutionalized as the Eucharistic Prayer celebrated in various forms and languages around the world today. Although the psalms and the Eucharist's Great Thanksgiving ground our liturgy, they are nevertheless only two of the many ways that define our communication with the Divine. The monastic prayers of the Daily Office, those offered as the Prayers of the People during the Liturgy of the Word, and the extemporaneous prayers in the privacy of our homes are only several examples. Despite this variety, however, it's the Eucharist that provides the most robust response to Jesus' disciples' request, "Lord, teach us to pray" (Luke 11.1a).

Anglican monk and liturgical theologian Dom Gregory Dix's magnum opus, *The Shape of the Liturgy* (2005), argues that the Eucharist comprises four distinct actions: taking, giving thanks, breaking, and sharing. Although his thesis has been critiqued by others in recent decades as overly simplistic and historically inadequate (if not inaccurate), it has survived as foundational for understanding the structure of Christian worship and prayer and as such merits our consideration of its potential application in the life we share as a community of faith.

Both the Eucharist and our personal prayers rightly begin with an offering—taking bread and wine to the altar, as well as recognizing the abundance of God's gifts and symbolically presenting them as the context for our Divine conversation. Each is an acknowledgment of the unbounded grace of God that makes our relationship with God even possible.

The late Swiss theologian Karl Barth noted the universal response to this generosity. "'Grace,' he said, 'evokes gratitude like the voice an echo.' Gratitude follows grace like thunder lightning" (2004). Whether humbled in awe by the presence of Christ's Body and Blood made real for us in the Mass or the utter amazement experienced reflecting on the depth of God's love and compassion, our unbridled thanksgiving is summoned as the only acceptable reaction.

The Eucharistic Prayer also is unflinchingly egalitarian. The breaking of the bread—whether loaf or wafer—enables the essence of the common offering to be shared with all. Although our individual prayers often reflect the unique needs of and hopes for our lives, they too provide a platform through which collective aspirations can be broken into discernable and relevant petitions for all within the community, a perspective clearly envisioned in The Book of Common Prayer's rubrics for the Prayers of the People (1979). The universal elements—the Church and its mission, the nation and those in authority, the welfare of the world, concerns of the local community, those who suffer, and the departed—are encouraged to be made particular to our own circumstances.

And finally, even as the Eucharist is accomplished through the sharing of Christ's Body and Blood and we're sent into the world to proclaim the Good News, so too must our prayers empower us to the ministry of the Gospel with all whose lives we might touch. To be sure, prayer is not mere meditation and a search for the soul of God; it's a call to action. Indeed, "For just as the body without the spirit is dead, so faith without works is dead" (James 2.26).

Individually and communally, we pray in many ways and employ any number of traditional and contemporary spiritual disciplines to guide us. As lay and clergy leaders of our parishes, we have several responsibilities for this dimension of Christian formation. First, it's critical that each of us engages in a routine of daily meditation, reflection on Scripture, and prayer. We truly need to model this for those we serve. Second, vestries and their clergy partners should lead congregational exploration of spiritual disciplines and prayer forms that excite the imagination, speak to the heart, and kindle the faith. And perhaps most challenging, we must engage our local communities in shared opportunities for interaction with the Divine.

Vestry Discussion

- Do you pray daily? If not, why not?
- Do you set aside a specific time and use a particular approach for your prayer life? If you do, how do those help to fulfill your spiritual life?
- What are the ways your congregation engages in organized prayer disciplines; for example, centering prayer?
- How might you facilitate a more robust prayer life among your parishioner?

Something to Ponder

Prayer and thanksgiving are at the core of the expression of the Christian faith. As we plumb the depths of our relationship with God, you're invited to spend time with the concept of "humble access." We come before God prostrate, confess our inadequacy and failures, and implore God's intervention, not because we deserve it but because we're accepted as we are—simply God's children.

"No Man Is an Island"

Opening Prayer

Loving God who shares the pain of our grief as we mourn loss in our lives: comfort us in the reality of life with those with whom we no longer share a physical journey; bind our community together in our grief and in our memories; give us the sure and certain hope of their resurrection and ours; and strengthen our resolve to continue their ministries in the Name of the risen Christ. Amen.

A Quote for Your Consideration

Since the disruption of the Garden of Eden's perfection, death and the grief that accompanies it have been inextricably embedded in the experience of all God's creatures. Consequently, it's no surprise that they should occupy such a prominent cultural position—ancient, as well as contemporary. Whether in the religious and social history of Israel,

Greece, and Rome; the literature of early Christianity, the Reformation, and Renaissance; or the scientific research of the past century, death and its impact have been explored for millennia. Although the context has typically been the effect of loss on an individual and the approaches for caring for them in their time of most profound mourning, death and grief also are communal experiences, beautifully memorialized in the poignant observation from seventeenth-century Anglican priest and poet John Donne (2002a):

> Here the bells can scare solemnize the funeral of any person, but that I knew him, or knew that he was my neighbor: we dwelt in houses near to one another before, but now he has gone into that house into which I must follow ... Who bends not his ear to any bell which upon any occasion rings? But who can remove it from that bell which is passing a piece of himself out of this world? No man is an island, entire of itself; every man is a piece of the continent, a part of the main. If a clod be washed away by the sea, Europe is the less, as well as if a promontory were, as well as if a manor of thy friend's or of thine own were: any man's death diminishes me, because I am involved in mankind, and therefore never send to know for whom the bell tolls; it tolls for thee.

Leadership in Context

Recently, after a long day hiking on the Beara Peninsula in southwestern Ireland and an evening of great pub food and Guinness, my wife and I enjoyed a leisurely morning and then began to look for a spot to indulge in a traditional breakfast. We walked into one that looked especially promising, scanned the menu which was tempting and then asked where we should take a seat. The owner looked at us quizzically as he told us that they would be closed for the next hour or so. Didn't we know there was a funeral this morning? Disappointed and hungry, we started walking down the street hoping to find somewhere to grab a bite. As we looked around, we noticed the doors to all the shops along the way were being closed, and people were beginning to line the sidewalk. We paused to take in the sight, not yet connecting the somber scene with the pending funeral. Then at a distance, we heard the muffled rumble of a hearse on the cobblestone road. Moments later, it passed by—a simple casket graced with flowers visible through its windows. But almost as quickly as this scene unfolded, doors along the way opened again and folks got on with their business. And, yes, we finally enjoyed a late breakfast—actually, an early lunch.

As we strolled through the quaint shops that afternoon, we had several conversations with the keepers about the funeral procession. We assumed that the deceased had been a person of some prominence given the incredible respect shown by the entire community. We soon learned, however, that the life honored was not that of a local luminary but just one of the townsfolk. In fact, the procession, shop closures and neighborly turnout were a longstanding tradition that we had the privilege to share.

The unexpected encounter with death and mourning in this quintessential Irish village has remained with me for many months—the respect, the simplicity, the ethereal quiet.

As I've processed it more fully, I've been reminded that while grief is experienced individually, it's shared communally. Each anniversary of the 9/11 terrorist attacks, for example, brings together spouses and children still grieving the loss of loved ones with an entire nation that shares their pain. The recent death of President Jimmy Carter was shared not only by his family and the residents of his native Plains, Georgia, but also with millions across the globe who grieved together as well. And local communities regularly turn out to support the families of fallen police officers, fire fighters, and paramedics. Indeed, death and grief are shared communally, most notably in the life of the Church. Yet, the preponderance of research has focused on individual loss.

Although philosophers of every age have reflected on death and its impact on survivors, it's not until the seventeenth century that they begin to be understood in the context of the emerging study of medicine as a science, particularly in what would become the field of psychiatry (Kelley 2010). The advent of psychoanalysis in the early twentieth century, however, laid the foundation for the subsequent analysis of grief and bereavement, importantly differentiating between purported "normal grief" and depression. The popularization of the stage theory of death and dying by Elizabeth Kubler-Ross—denial, anger, bargaining, depression, and acceptance—further advanced the intellectual framework for research. Yet, despite the importance of these contributions, it's recently become increasingly clear that grief is a complex tapestry that varies greatly among individuals.

Although the literature on collective grief is less well-developed, it appears to define two layers of experience—the specific responses of individuals to their losses, as well as the overlay of an entire group sharing these many different experiences simultaneously. So, for example, during the COVID-19 pandemic, many of us knew people who died from this ubiquitous virus. We mourned their loss and engaged long-standing religious and secular rituals to help focus our grief and engender hope. However, as the death toll mounted into the hundreds of thousands across the nation, we emotionally connected—millions of us—in lamenting loss, searching for meaning, and grasping for a hope that would ease our pain even as restrictions on funerals limited our access to community.

Jesus' disciples likely found themselves in the same place in the three days following his crucifixion. Each had a unique relationship with him in the years they traveled together, and I suspect each mourned his death in a particularly personal way. Although Scripture reveals little about this brief time, Mark's Gospel notes that the disciples "were mourning and weeping" (16.10), while John's informs us that "the doors were locked where the disciples were, for fear . . ." (20.19a). The uncertainty that clearly enveloped them, the unimaginable transition from Jesus' triumphant entry into Jerusalem to the isolation of Golgotha and a profound sense of abandonment would have been understandable emotions. So, too, might have been their collective response—gathering rather than each remaining alone, processing their loss together and praying.

As communities of faith, we regularly find ourselves in a similar situation as we individually and communally grieve the death of beloved siblings in Christ. Although we're generally adept at the rituals accompanying death, the pastoral care of immediate family and close friends, and the conduct of funerals and the receptions that often follow, we too quickly move on. To be sure, individual memories and stories are shared, but seldom do we structure conversations among the entire parish family to discuss the specific impact of and emotions resulting from the loss of an integral member of our community.

While the evangelists don't offer a comprehensive perspective on the effects of grief shared in community or strategies for coping with them, their few observations are consistent with contemporary scholarship. It's vital that clergy and vestries provide a robust infrastructure for congregational grieving, including not only the various activities surrounding a funeral but also provisions for the members of the parish collectively to reflect on the impact of the loss on the community. Ensuring that the congregation can remain bonded around the loss of one of its own also is vitally important. For example, service projects reflecting the deceased's interests and ministries might be organized to memorialize their contributions to the congregation. Additionally, structuring specific activities in conjunction with All Saints' and All Souls' Days, such as a reception, concert, or lecture, offers the opportunity for the faithful and faithful departed to remain connected. Regardless of the approaches, however, facilitating the ability of the community to grieve together, as well as enabling the grief itself to shape the community, are fundamental to being the Church.

Vestry Discussion

- What role (if any) has your faith community played in helping you cope with grief from the losses you've experienced? Was it helpful? Why or why not?
- What more could be done within your faith community to assist individuals with their grief?
- What more could be done within your congregation to recognize and respond to the communal grief experienced because of a death or other losses?

Something to Ponder

Death and other significant losses are a reality of life. As we consider how best to fully embrace those who are grieving with the Gospel of Jesus Christ and certainty of the Resurrection, you're invited to reflect on "mourning." What individual and collective practices might best facilitate a healthy response to the emotional trauma of loss?

"Do Not Be Afraid"

Opening Prayer

Lord God of courage and strength beyond all measure: temper our anxieties amid the vagaries of this world; quell our fear of those we do not know, understand or with whom we disagree; calm our concerns in the face of changes seemingly beyond our control; and raise your might against all who might harm your people and creation. For your mercy's sake, we pray. Amen.

A Quote for Your Consideration

We live in a world in which fear abounds. Fear of war, pain, suffering, and death. Fear of "the other." Fear of inadequacy and failure. And fear of uncertainty and change. Our congregations clearly are not immune. We often find ourselves afraid of the winds of cultural change that sweep over our parishes. We fear for the ability to sustain ministry to one another, as well as the larger community we serve. And we regularly find ourselves desperate to overcome the anxieties that accompany our personal and professional lives.

As we summoned in the opening prayer, courage—God's and ours—is at the very heart of confronting fear. Theologians Stanley Hauerwas and Charles Pinches address its essential merit, as well as the limitations to what it can accomplish (Hauerwas and Pinches 2001):

> Courage and temperance are the virtues that form what Aristotle assumed were our most basic appetites: fear and pleasure. The purpose is not to repress these appetites but to form them to function rightly. Hence courage does not eliminate fear—that would be recklessness. Rather, courage forms us to have fear in the right amount, at the right time, about the right things, and so on.

Leadership in Context

It's early October. Here in Colorado, the Aspen leaves shimmer in the wind as they're beginning to change from lush green to vibrant yellow gold. Just days ago, the High Country experienced its first snow of the season. And hope springs eternal among the football faithful who eagerly anticipate gridiron glory for the Denver Broncos and University of Colorado Buffalos.

My thoughts, however, have tended to drift toward the fear that seems to have gripped the American psyche these days. Hurricane Helene devastated Florida and the East Coast as far north as Appalachia. And even as recovery efforts are underway, folks are bracing for more havoc before the winds and seas calm later in the fall. Mass shootings at street parties and high schools—not to mention two assassination attempts on a former president—have left many reeling, hunkering down in fear, and, tragically, buying more guns. And then there's the national election in which both sides are stoking apocalyptic fear should the other prevail at the polls.

Although fear manifests in specific contexts and moments in time, it's in fact elemental to the human condition and essential for our survival. The "fight or flight" response to real threats engendered by fear is a fully rational and appropriate reaction to forces that portend harm. However, baseless anxiety and fear frequently disrupt the orderly functioning of our lives and society—all too often paralyzing our ability to understand complex situations and marshal an informed response to them.

With fears of all sorts (real or imagined) widespread among the community we serve, the nation we treasure, and even our own congregants, how might we understand and respond to them with the empathy and love of the Gospel? To be sure, this is an almost overwhelming challenge, but perhaps we might manage it by considering the typical sources of our fear.

Among the most prevalent is the fear of change—in our life circumstances, in our relationships, in the way we worship. Although adaptability has marked the human experience from the beginning of creation, we seem rather quickly to become entrenched in whatever new reality has emerged. So, for example, many of us dread the departure of our children as they enter young adulthood but also soon come to relish "empty nester" status and new-found freedoms. Likewise, neighbors and friends tie us to our communities and understandably often factor in relocation decisions. Yet, as most of us have learned, longstanding relationships can be maintained (albeit at a distance) even as new ones are formed. And for those in positions of congregational leadership, change—especially in the format and content of worship—can be particularly disruptive but eventually can emerge as liberating.

I'm reminded of two congregations that consolidated several years ago, one with a rich history of Episcopal liturgy and sensibilities and the other struggling with its identity. Despite years of diocesan support and each parish cobbling together resources to maintain their ministries, neither could any longer sustain themselves, and a merger offered the only realistic hope for a continued presence in the community. However, the prospect of change—in location, in name, in liturgical style, and so much more—fomented fear in both congregations. People balked, some left, and still others actively attempted to undermine the merger. Today, however, a new and vibrant congregation has emerged and taken its place as a significant voice in the work of the diocese and a leader in the economically distressed community it serves, none of which could have been accomplished without the leadership of the vestry, the consolidated congregation's new rector, and the diocese's bishop.

Nationally, the violent political rhetoric that has swept across America in the past decade reflects a historic pattern of demonizing "the other" and fueling fear of those different from us whom we don't understand (or even try to). However, this is nothing new. Israel's embattled relationships with the many tribes of the Ancient Near East, Jesus' encounter with the Syrophoenician woman, and the rejection of the wounded traveler on the road to Jericho by a priest and Levite (only to be eventually comforted by a much-despised Samaritan) attest to our discomfort with and hostility toward those whose ethnicity, religion, culture, wealth, social status, or politics differ from ours. Our country's response to the waves of immigrants from southern and eastern Europe and Asia, the internment of Americans of Japanese descent during World War II, and the Islamophobia in the wake of the 9/11 terrorist attack punctuate that several millennia later we're not immune to the same fears and prejudice. Not only do these fears undermine the democratic ideals and social contract of our society, but they also frequently encroach on the lives we share together as communities of faith. How many congregations, for example, have been divided over issues of race, sexual identity, or the proclamation of a "too politically partisan" Gospel from the pulpit? Again, the prophetic leadership of the vestry and clergy is pivotal in redirecting fear into a broader understanding, acceptance, and mutual respect.

The importance of pastoral care and congregational governance deeply rooted in the boundless love of Christ was reflected in the mid-twentieth-century history of a parish I know well. A new rector arrived to serve this prominent, well-educated, and predominantly white congregation, but sadly on his first Sunday in the pulpit he noticed that the Black people attending the worship service were all seated in the back pews. I'm told that he summoned the vestry to a meeting the following day and informed them that he would not serve another unless worship was integrated and Black participants were fully welcomed into the life of this faith community. The uncompromising demand was met, and this parish became one of the leading institutions in the desegregation of the community, a role it continues to champion to this day.

Both the fear of change and "the other" share a common origin: uncertainty and our inability to control the future fully. The challenge for vestries and clergy is to recognize the reality of the fears people experience and even when misguided or hateful to understand them, with the hope of engaging them in the unfettered embrace of a God who invites the conversion of their lives. This is no easy task, and the path can be treacherous for all. But it's work that must be done, and clergy and vestries are summoned to lead in challenging the fears that disrupt our lives and the pastoral reach of our congregations.

Although daunting, the voice of the Lord's angel speaking to terrified shepherds from the skies over Bethlehem reminded them and us today, "Do not be afraid, for see, I am bringing you good news of great joy for all the people: to you is born this day in the city of David a Savior, who is the Messiah, the Lord" (Luke 2.10–11). Indeed, we need not fear anything or for want of anything, for the redemption of the world has been secured for all time in Christ Jesus, a point eloquently shared by sixteenth-century Anglican bishop Edwin Sandys (2002):

> But the Spirit of adoption by the preaching of the gospel telleth us that in Christ we have remission of sins; we are reconciled unto God, and adopted by him; we are his chosen children, and may boldly and joyfully call him Father. And this certainty of our salvation the Spirit of God testifieth to our spirit, whereby we put away all servile fear of punishment, being assured of God's constant favour and eternal love towards us; who never leaveth unfinished that which he hath begun, nor forsaketh him whom he hath chosen.

Vestry Discussion

- What do you most fear and how has it impacted your life?
- How do you overcome fear? Is there a spiritual discipline that's especially helpful?
- What fears have manifested in your parish? Did the clergy and vestry respond? If so, how and with what results? If not, why and with what results?

- What might the vestry and clergy do to cultivate a culture of hope for the parish and its members, the community they serve, and the world we inhabit?

Something to Ponder

The uncertainty often embodied in fear provides an opportunity for us to reflect on the foundation of our faith and how it transforms distress into hope. You're invited to consider "courage" as a particularly important dimension of our Christian character in response to the fears—real or imagined—experienced by all for whom we care.

"Why Have You Forsaken Me?"

Opening Prayer

Lord God, in whose infinite mercy we dwell: from the depths of our darkness, shed light on our path; from the loneliness and alienation that dampen our spirits, bolster us with your Presence; from the depression that gnaws at our soul, heal us; and from the valley of despair that defies explanation, give us hope. In Jesus' Name, we pray. Amen.

A Quote for Your Consideration

Why me? Why this? Why now? I doubt any of us have escaped the emotional and spiritual trauma that accompanies devastating news or tragic circumstances. In confronting a shattering medical diagnosis, the struggle with fractured family relationships, or the loss of a job or loved one, it's understandable that our lives often seem to spin out of control. Love is stretched, our sense of community and belonging trampled, and our faith difficult to maintain, if at all. The resulting despair has the capacity to immobilize every fiber of our being. Yet, we are not unique in our experience nor alone despite our inability to comprehend or rationalize the overwhelming situations that inevitably attempt to hold us hostage. In grappling with his own cancer diagnosis, the late John A. T. Robinson, Bishop of Woolwich and provocative New Testament scholar, shared a heartfelt perspective on faith's response to the propensity for despair in the darkest moments of our lives (2001):

> The other question people ask in such circumstances is "Why me?" (often with the implication, "Why does he pick on me?") or "What have I done to deserve it?" And this deep down, is another good question to have out. "Why have I got this? What is there in me that has brought it about?" To which the answer is for the most part, as in so much in this field, "I don't know." Certainly it is in my case. But the searching, probing and often uncomfortable questions it raises are very relevant, and can be an essential part of the healing.

Leadership in Context

I'm usually very attentive to anniversaries—both personal and public ... joyful and painful. September 6 (my wedding anniversary) and March 7 (my wife's birthday) are easily remembered even without a calendar. So too are December 7,

November 22, and 9/11. Yet this morning, I found myself lamenting that somehow the anniversary of the December 14, 2014, slaughter of children and their teachers at Sandy Hook Elementary School had slipped by. I wondered whether I, like so many, had become desensitized to the gun violence that plagues our country like none other in the world or just got caught up in the frenzy of the holidays. As I returned home from the day's errands, however, I turned on the television to check the news at noon only to learn of the tragic shooting of students and teachers at a nondenominational Christian school in Madison, Wisconsin. I paused—stunned—sank into a chair and muttered, "How could this be happening again ... and again ... and again?" Then I prayed. "God, where are you?"

The sense that in the depths of our confusion and pain God has abandoned us is a theme that resounds throughout Scripture. David's plea in Psalm 22.1, "My God, my God, why have you forsaken me?" and echoed by Jesus on the cross (Matthew 27.46) speaks to the desolation so often experienced by those confronting the reality of their own death. Job (3.1–26) also gives voice to his perceived abandonment by God and increasing despair. And among the most powerful expressions of hopeless recorded in Scripture is John's recounting of Mary Magdelene at Jesus' tomb (John 20.11–13):

> But Mary stood weeping outside the tomb. As she wept, she bent over to look into the tomb, and she saw two angels in white, sitting where the body of Jesus had been lying, one at the head and the other at the feet. They said to her, "Woman, why are you weeping?" She said to them, "They have taken away

my Lord, and I do not know where they have laid him."

So recurrent is the theme of despair in both the Hebrew Scriptures and the New Testament that it's been the subject of theological inquiry across millennia and religious traditions. The Covenant between God and the people of Israel grounds Judaism's repeated struggle with misfortune—betrayals, wars, and exiles to name but a few—in the hope that their return to faithfulness will merit God's mercy and relieve their anguish. Roman Catholicism has long understood despair to be a human failure in which we're unable to accept God's unbridled grace and forgiveness and, therefore, descend further into sin's eternal pit. Although many of the Protestant reformers of the sixteenth and seventeenth centuries share the personal culpability for despair with the Church of Rome, they emphasize God's connection to our suffering, how we mature spiritually amid it and more deeply engage our faith—reaching a point of self-acceptance in the sight of God. But for those of us in the Anglican tradition, the concept of "kenosis" (self-emptying) perhaps best describes our understanding of despair and response to it, a theological perspective most closely associated with Orthodox theologians of the past century. As Christ emptied himself on the cross, so too are we invited to shed our concerns at its foot. In giving himself totally to God, he was lifted to eternal life. So, as we empty ourselves into God's hands even in the most tragic circumstances, we also inherit the fullness of God's love and mercy.

In addition to the Biblical record of despair among the people of God, contemporary psychological theory also has explored it, summarized succinctly by the late psychotherapist Paul W. Pruyser (2005):

> Hoping is a realistic and adaptive response to extreme stress or crisis in which the person acquires a patient and confident surrender to uncontrollable, transcendent forces ... Similarly, despair may be regarded as a more objectless and profound depressed state than, for example, grief, which attaches to specific loss. Despair and hope are better seen as in complex dialectical relation than as simple antonyms.

Whether understood primarily through a theological or psychological lens, both share common elements in addressing despair. Fundamental is the hope that its cause can be reversed, as evidenced by research on those who survived Nazi concentration camps or potentially mortal illnesses. Confidence that human goodness and science will ultimately prevail in these challenging circumstances grounds secular thought. Alternatively, the sure and certain trust in God's mercy and redemptive power secured through Jesus' death and resurrection are central to Christian faith, even amid our most difficult struggles.

Jesus models a second element essential to our response to despair—prayer—most notably in his plea to God on the Mount of Olives before his arrest, trial, and crucifixion. "Father, if you are willing, remove this cup from me; yet not my will but yours be done" (Luke 22.42). It's hard to imagine a more profound example of self-emptying than this poignant moment. Likewise, focused and deep reflection can measurably contribute to emotional and psychological healing.

Finally, we're reminded that even in the depths of despair, we're not alone. A community of faith embraces us. And we pray as well that all whom we hold most dear rally around us.

Certainly, each of us individually has experienced moments of hopelessness, powerlessness, and despair. So, too, have vestries. Buildings in continual need of maintenance and repairs, only some of which were projected in the budget. Staff turnover that so disrupts programming and operations. And community initiatives that seemingly make no dent in the problems of our own neighborhood illustrate challenges we all too often find overwhelming. Yet, the Psalmist reminds us, "I lift up my eyes to the hills—from where will my help come? My help comes from the Lord, who made heaven and earth" (Psalm 121.1–2). In those moments when darkness seems to blot out the light of hope, I also invite you to take a moment to view the YouTube music video of the Hanukkah rendition of "Rise Up" by the Jewish male *a cappella* group Y-Studs, formed in 2010 at New York's Yeshiva University. The magic of their voices and the force of the lyrics can't help but lift your spirit and give you hope. Rise up, ye faithful!

Vestry Discussion

- How have you experienced hopelessness and despair in your life?
- What resources were most helpful in coping with despair? What didn't seem to help?

- What challenges are confronting your parish that appear to be intractable, if any?
- What can your vestry do to further a culture of hope and trust within your faith community?

Something to Ponder

Loneliness, alienation, powerlessness, and despair are emotions locked into the human experience and known to all of us at various points in our lives. Our faith summons us to trust in God's work among us in the most troubling moments. And in doing so, you're encouraged to consider "hope"—its source and the role it plays in your life.

FAITH'S JOURNEY THROUGHOUT THE YEAR

Advent's Question: How Could This Be?

Opening Prayer

God of infinite grace and love: fulfill the desires of hearts that long for you; quench the thirst of those who search for your knowledge; feed those who hunger for your wisdom; bless those who share your mercy; and bring joy to all who see your glory made present in your Son, Jesus the Messiah. Amen.

A Quote for Your Consideration

The expectation of the coming of an incarnate God defines our understanding of Advent and frames our experience of it. We wait. We wonder. And we hope. Especially for long-time churchgoers, it seems awkward that we spiritually suspend time each year, return to the world of ancient Israel, and pray for the Messiah promised by the prophets. After all, we know the Christmas narrative! Yet, it's essential that we annually journey with Jesus from Bethlehem to Golgotha and Galilee. Not only does it remind us of the pivotal moments of his life and ministry, but it also reinforces the walk we must share with him—every moment of every day. As we prepare for it, you're invited to consider the following quote from Episcopal priest and author Barbara Brown Taylor (1998):

> On the one hand [Mary] was just a girl, an immature and frightened girl who had the good sense to believe what an angel told her in what seemed like a dream. On the other hand, she was the mother of the Son of God, with faith enough to move mountains, to sing about the victories of her son as if he were already at the right hand of his father instead of a dollop of cells in her womb.... When we allow God to be born in us, there is no telling, no telling at all, what will come out.

Leadership in Context

"How can this be?" (Luke 1.34) exclaimed a startled and confused Mary at the angel Gabriel's announcement that she will bear the "Son of the Most High." After all, she was young, just recently engaged, and had not consummated the relationship with her fiancé, Joseph. This is not a unique reaction in the annals of the Biblical narrative. Moses wasn't all that keen on leading the Israelites out of Egypt nor Jeremiah becoming God's prophet. But in confronting news of an improbable birth that must have been truly shocking, Mary gives voice to a question echoed by so many of us when events seemingly defy explanation.

How can it be, for example, that more than 45,000 of our neighbors have been lost to gun violence in the past year? How can it be that marriages fail, children are trafficked, and friends die? How can it be that companies are reorganized, jobs placed in jeopardy, and dreams left in ruin? And how can it be that our hopes so often seem little more than airbrushed fantasies? Lord, how can this be?

Even our congregations are not immune to shock and reversals. How can it be that stewardship initiatives fall short despite our most intense and creative efforts? How can it be that clergy move on from the wonderful faith community we have nurtured together? And how can it be that the liturgical traditions we remember so fondly somehow no longer seem important to those who organize our worship? Lord, how can this be?

The Season of Advent focuses our attention on the improbable, the unexpected, and the unwanted. Confusing though these can be, Mary's conversation with Gabriel and her ultimate response to the call to Divine motherhood provide us with the guidance we need to navigate such troubled waters. Initially confounded, Mary quickly informed an apparently ignorant Gabriel of a fundamental impediment to human procreation—namely, she's a virgin! Nevertheless, he would have none of it. But rather than dismissing her concerns, Gabriel reoriented them. The birth will be God's doing. The Holy Spirit will come upon her. And the power of the "Lord God" will overshadow her. The message is clear. As perplexing and complicated as Mary's task will be, God will sustain her.

Despite the improbability of God's challenge channeled through Gabriel, Mary responded with the glorious refrain, "Here am I, the servant of the Lord; let it be with me according to your word" (Luke 1.38a). Her misgivings notwithstanding, Mary simply and directly accepted her commission as an agent of God.

Whether in our personal lives or in the leadership of our congregations, what are we to make of this implausible story? How are we to interpret Mary's faithfulness and joy even amid a significant crisis? And what is there about Mary's response to uncertainty and likely public ridicule that might comfort and strengthen us in our moments of deepest despair?

Perhaps most important, we're to understand the particularity of Gabriel's announcement to Mary. Although we often reflect on Christ's presence in the world we inhabit, Gabriel reminds us that Christ is distinctively and uniquely present in each of us. He shares our hopes and fears, our pains and expectations, our losses and grief. And he hears our cry—"How can this be?"—and is moved by it. Also, even as Mary is reassured by God's promise shared by Gabriel, she's challenged to reach beyond herself and beyond her fear to bear witness of God's immeasurable grace to the entire world. It's no easy task to which she was summoned . . . nor is it for us. Wounded though we may be, we're empowered by the promise of the Christ to hear God's grace, to be transformed by it, and to reach out to all whose lives we might touch. To those in need of food, shelter, or health care. To those struggling in pain, aching in spirit, or nearing the end of their days. And to all those simply in need of a place of safety and forgiveness.

Truly, this is the challenge for our lives and the leadership of our parishes—to hear God's call to us, to overcome our skepticism and concern, and to offer ourselves in the service of the God who has invited us to join in the proclamation of the Good News of Jesus Christ. Even as we struggle with the

"How can this be?" moments in our personal and communal lives, may we join Mary in celebrating God's work in and among us.

> My soul magnifies the Lord, and my spirit rejoices in God my Savior, for he has looked with favor on the lowly state of his servant. Surely, from now on all generations will call me blessed; for the Mighty One has done great things for me, and holy is his name. His mercy is for those who fear him from generation to generation. He has shown strength with his arm; he has scattered the proud in the thoughts of their hearts. He has brought down the powerful from their thrones, and lifted up the lowly; he has filled the hungry with good things, and sent the rich away empty. He has helped his servant Israel, in remembrance of his mercy, according to the promise he made to our ancestors, to Abraham and to his descendants forever (Luke 1.46b–55).

Vestry Discussion

- What is worrying you now and seems beyond explanation and resolution?
- How do you respond to desperate situations that appear to be beyond control? What role does your spiritual life play in addressing them?
- What seemingly insoluble issue(s) is currently causing consternation or struggle within your congregation or vestry?

- How might Mary's encounter with Gabriel and response to God's call inform your approach to the "How can this be?" moments in your faith community?

Something to Ponder

Amid a world in crisis and our lives too frequently upended, we often find ourselves grappling with the inexplicable and straining to find a path forward. The encounter between Mary and Gabriel provides a model resolution of circumstances we don't fully comprehend. Consequently, you're invited to reflect on the meaning of "struggle" and how to engage God in understanding difficult situations and addressing them.

"In the Beginning Was the Word": Christmas' Proclamation

Opening Prayer

God of humble majesty who became one of us through the birth of your Son Jesus, the Messiah: enter our lives anew with your redemptive grace; open the world to the Good News of the Gospel; touch all in fear, pain, or distress with your healing Presence; and lift our voices rejoicing in the gift of the Incarnation. All for your love's sake. Amen.

A Quote for Your Consideration

Jesus' life and ministry are framed by two pivotal events in which he "breaks into" the world. An empty tomb with its stone rolled away, the angelic declaration that "he [Jesus] is not here" (Matthew 28.6a), and his post-Resurrection appearances mark Jesus' triumphant victory over death and his return to live with us eternally. Likewise, Jesus' meek birth in the backwaters of Judea attests to God's entering creation dramatically—becoming incarnate. As we prepare to celebrate Christmas and the remarkable birth of the Christ, the voice of seventeenth-century Anglican priest and poet John Donne speaks glowingly of God becoming human (2002b):

> If some king of the earth have so large an extent of dominion in north and south, as that he hath winter and summer together in his dominions, so large an extent east and west, as that he hath day and night together in his dominions, much more hath God mercy and judgment together: he brought light out of darkness, not out of a lesser light; he can bring thy summer out of winter, though thou have no spring; though in the ways of fortune, or understanding, or conscience, thou have been benighted till now, wintered and frozen, clouded and eclipsed, dampened and benumbed, smothered and stupefied till now, now God comes to thee, not as in the dawning of the day, not as in the bud of the spring, but as the sun at noon, to illumine all shadows, as the sheaves in harvest, to fill all penuries. All occasions invite his mercies, and all times are his seasons.

Leadership in Context

The very first words I read in my undergraduate class in Biblical Greek in 1970 were from the prologue to the Gospel of John. "In the beginning was the Word, and the Word was with God, and the Word was God" (1.1). I doubt I had previously spent much time considering the evangelist's use of "Word" (*Logos* in Greek) to describe God. At that time in my life, it was simply a familiar Sunday school phrase and the initial step in the mastery of a new language. In the decades that followed, however, I've routinely found myself delving more deeply into John's introductory verses as I've tried to grasp the reality of God, especially during Christmastide:

> In the beginning was the Word, and the Word was with God, and the Word was God. He was in the beginning with God. All things came into being through him, and without him not one thing came into being. What has come into being in him was life, and the life was the light of all people.
>
> The light shines in the darkness, and the darkness did not overcome it. There was a man sent from God, whose name was John. He came as a witness to testify to the light, so that all might believe through him. He himself was not the light, but he came to testify to the light. The true light, which enlightens everyone, was coming into the world. He was in the world, and the world came into being through him; yet the world did not know him. He came to what was his own, and his own people did not accept him. But to all who received him, who believed in his name, he gave power to become children of God, who were born, not of blood or of the will of the flesh or of the will of man, but of God. And the Word became flesh and

lived among us, and we have seen his glory, the glory as of a father's only son, full of grace and truth. (John testified to him and cried out, "This was he of whom I said, 'He who comes after me ranks ahead of me because he was before me.'") From his fullness we have all received, grace upon grace. The law indeed was given through Moses; grace and truth came through Jesus Christ. No one has ever seen God. It is the only Son, who is close to the Father's heart, who has made him known (John 1.1–18).

The prologue to John's Gospel begins with the bold assertion that God has always been—from before the "Big Bang"... even from before time. And then, he declares that the Word, Jesus, was always with God and, in fact, is God. And like God, there was never a time when Jesus was not. Importantly, John would have us understand that all of creation—all of life—flows from and through this God in whom Jesus is fully embedded.

So, creation is the expression of God's control over all that is and Jesus, from the very beginning, is a full and equal partner in setting God's agenda for the world. However, despite the clarity of John's proclamation, he anticipated that some would disagree or, at the very least, need further evidence. Toward that end, God appointed John the Baptist—the latest in a long line of Jewish prophets—not only to proclaim the fullness of God but to announce God's pending entrance into the human experience in the person of Jesus. This was not to be some magical appearance orchestrated by a divine Wizard of Oz. Far from it! Rather, the birth of Jesus was to confirm and punctuate the inseparable relationship between God and all that has been created, including the world and lives we inhabit.

One would have assumed that John's announcement that "The true light, which enlightens everyone, was coming into the world" (John 1.9) would have been met with universal enthusiasm and joy. But clearly, that was not to be the case. We can almost hear John's anguish as he relates the response of so many to Jesus. "He came to what was his own, and his own people did not accept him" (John 1.11). How painful to be rejected by your own children!

Yet, despite the refusal of so many to embrace the fullness of God in Jesus, John reminds us that some indeed did. And for them, their belief was life-changing. They were invited to become one with God. And in becoming one, they were redeemed. Thus, in the span of the eighteen verses of the prologue, John has woven together the two fundamental narratives of Scripture: creation and salvation. The God of creation and the God of redemption are one. We are brought into the life of God because God entered ours.

The theological import of John's prologue is as profound as it is dense. There's no signal of the ministry Jesus is to embrace—nothing of miracles, healing, parables, or disciples. Rather, the text is precisely as it's described, a prelude laying the foundation for the story to be told. However, that doesn't mean it's bereft of specific insights for our Christmas reflections, prayers, and hymns.

Particularity is at the very heart of the Incarnation. God is not an amorphous spirit, a shapeless manifestation of the Divine. Rather, in Jesus we encounter a specific man who would mesmerize crowds with his preaching, heal their sores with his touch, and weep at the loss of his friend Lazarus. It's also the same Jesus who would be betrayed, suffer, be crucified and then be resurrected. While rightfully Christmas is a time of great joy, John's prologue also is a reminder that Good Friday and Easter are on the horizon. To comprehend God made flesh in Jesus—God becoming one of us—is to accept that the experience will be full, it will be complete, and it will embrace both life and death.

But it's not just that his death and resurrection have secured our own eternal life. It's in the small details of Jesus' life and ministry that we come to know both the depth and breadth of God. A God of immeasurable love. A God of uncompromising faithfulness. And a God of eternal grace and mercy. Indeed, just as the Incarnation enables our redemption, so too does it reveal the God who occasions it (Long 2008).

Unlike the other reflections in this book, there's no vestry "to do list" for this one. Rather, you're invited simply to bask in the joy of God's becoming human, the implications of the Incarnation for the world, and its meaning in our ministries and the lives of all we might touch. May this joy give you hope for the year ahead!

Vestry Discussion

- How do you understand the relationship between the incarnation of God in Jesus and the redemption secured by his death and resurrection?
- What experiences and traditions of Christmastide have most shaped your faith and brought you joy?

- Especially for those for whom the holiday season is difficult, if not painful, how might you and your parish embrace them with the joy of Jesus' birth?

Something to Ponder

Christmas brings with it a breadth of emotions for the faithful, as well as for those who struggle with or reject it. As you reflect on the gift of the Christ, you're invited to consider what it means for Jesus to be "the light of all people" (John 1.4b).

Lost in Epiphany's Shuffle

Opening Prayer

Gracious God, who daily lifts the veil of darkness that clouds our vision of the kingdom made present in your Son, Jesus Christ: map the path of our journey with him; light our way; give us courage to face all that we will encounter; and grant us the sure hope of life forever in your embrace. All for your love's sake. Amen.

A Quote for Your Consideration

OK. Be honest. The season of Epiphany is not likely at the forefront of our personal calendars as we ease into the new year. We barely shake off Christmas tree needles, sweep up gift wrappings, and rebalance our diets before we're well into this time when we begin to explore Jesus as truly the Son of God through his baptism, early ministry, and transfiguration.

And sadly, for too many of us, our celebration of Epiphany and all that it exposes is limited to remembering the travels of three wise men from a distant land who followed a radiant star and brought gifts to the baby Jesus. Yet, these few weeks between Christmastide and Lent are essential in preparation for our journey with him, a passage that will reveal the shining brilliance of God Incarnate, as well as provide a glimpse of the darkness we'll share with him en route to the cross. The twentieth-century Archbishop of Canterbury and champion of social justice William Temple offered wise counsel and encouragement for engaging the fullness of the Epiphany season (2002b):

> As we look forward, we peer into darkness, and none can say with certainty what course the true progress of the future should follow. But as we look back, the truth is marked by beacon-lights, which are the lives of the saints and pioneers; and these in their turn are not originators of light, but rather reflectors which give light to us, because they themselves are turned to the source of light ... The redemption of man is part, even if the crowning part, of a greater thing, the redemption, or conquest, of the universe. Till that be accomplished the darkness abides, pierced but unilluminated by the beam of divine light. And the one great question for everyone is whether he will "walk in darkness" or "walk in the light."

Leadership in Context

Matthew's recounting of three magi—historically dubbed Melchior, Caspar, and Balthazar—who traveled from the East following a particularly glowing star to see Jesus is a staple of the extended birth narrative (Matthew 2.1–23). Although often referenced as kings, they likely were astrologers whose practice was to study the nighttime skies and search for meaning in the location and movement of solar objects. Somehow, they divined that a child had been born as "king of the Jews" and eventually made their way to Bethlehem bearing precious gifts for Jesus, the Messiah—gold, frankincense, and myrrh.

For most of us, this is a treasured story from our childhood memorialized in hymns, pageants, and chalking our front doors. However, the emphasis on the wise men and their gifts too often obscures the complexity of their visit and its place within the larger story. There's much more for us to consider individually and as leaders of our congregations.

Although Matthew (2.2) informs us that these astrologers observed "his [Jesus'] star at its rising" as it guided them, there's no further mention of this bright light. Yet, it's at the very heart of the Epiphany feast. It's the representative manifestation of Christ, the Messiah, breaking into the world as one of us—fully and truly human. It signals that the world will never again be the same. And it reflects the absolute glow of the Father making his Divine Presence known to all.

But the star's primary function was to light a path, guide a journey, and mark a destination. Certainly, this goal was accomplished. And in doing so, it also directs us on a journey with Jesus from Bethlehem's manger to Golgotha's cross and an empty tomb in a nearby garden. We're reminded daily that as we live into our faith and share it with a world so much in need of the Good News, it's the radiance of the

Christ—first revealed in the intense glow of a star—that orients our way and enables us to experience the fullness of the Lord. Additionally, it's this same bright light that reminds us of the parish leadership in which we're engaged, focuses us on the consistent application of our vision, mission, and values, and guides our deliberations.

When the magi arrived at the stable, they found Jesus in a manger surrounded by his parents and animals. Now, a manger is a V-shaped wooden farm implement used to hold hay, keep it dry, and allow animals to feed from it easily. The problem with the birth narrative, however, is that the newborn baby Jesus occupied the manger, with the surrounding animals seemingly left to scrounge for dinner. We can only assume (and hope) that this was simply an editorial oversight and that none of the sheep, donkeys, or camels went hungry. Nevertheless, the scene in the stable is a prescient reminder of the flock that needs to be tended.

It seems to me that's where the shepherds come in. Although not mentioned in Matthew's Gospel, they are in Luke's narrative (2.15–18):

> When the angels had left them and gone into heaven, the shepherds said to one another, "Let us go now to Bethlehem and see this thing that has taken place, which the Lord has made known to us." So they went with haste and found Mary and Joseph, and the child lying in the manger. When they saw this, they made known what had been told them about this child; and all who heard it were amazed at what the shepherds told them.

It's inconceivable that they would have come down from the hills without the sheep in their charge. Their lives in the countryside were tough—bandits, the vagaries of the weather, and sheep who frequently wandered off on their own. Nonetheless, shepherds knew how to cope, keep their sheep safe, and lead them to food and water. They brought these same talents to the stable, and we can easily imagine that they took the lead in providing the necessary provisions for both their charges and the animals already gathered around Jesus.

While perhaps taking a bit of whimsical liberty with these texts, the circumstances of the animals and shepherds remind us of the servant leadership to which we've been called. Jesus didn't break into the world simply to be worshipped and glorified or to be a remote deity inaccessible to the faithful. Rather the scene in the stable acknowledges that there are many who will need to be fed with food and water, but more importantly with the joyful news of the Incarnation. The care and comfort of all whose lives we might touch has, from the beginning of Jesus' life, been the unequivocal expectation of the faithful, especially the clergy and vestries who lead them.

The Feast of the Epiphany and the weeks that follow are replete with "glad tidings," Jesus' public presentation and the works of his early ministry. However, there's also a sense of foreboding hanging over this otherwise jubilant time, reported in the second chapter of Matthew. Even before discovering Jesus in Bethlehem, the magi were engaged by a jealous king Herod in a conspiratorial attempt to locate his rival and likely be rid of him. The plot thickened when the wise men were warned in a dream to avoid him, returning to their home by a secondary route. Likewise, an angel summoned Mary and Joseph to leave Bethlehem with their newborn child and relocate to Egypt. Frustrated by their elusiveness, Herod ruthlessly murdered all the children under two years of age in and around Bethlehem, hoping that such an indiscriminate slaughter would at least snare the purported "king of the Jews." Even after Herod's death and an angel's command to return to Israel, the family had to alter their route to avoid his son, Archelaus, finally settling in the Galilean town of Nazareth.

Thus, as we bask in the joy of this season, we're confronted with the undercurrent of violence and death to which Jesus will ultimately succumb, so poignantly captured in the Epiphany hymn (#128, v.4) *We Three Kings of Orient Are*:

> Myrrh is mine; its bitter perfume
> breathes a life of gathering gloom;
> sorrowing, sighing, bleeding, dying,
> sealed in the stone-cold tomb.

To be sure, our lives and congregational leadership will span the full experience of this season—from unmitigated joy to the depths of sadness, confusion, and grief. Yet even as we journey with him toward the inexorable conclusion of his incarnation, we'll be guided by the same stellar brilliance that brought the wise men, shepherds, and us to him. And we also know that this same star will light the way to Easter's empty tomb. May Epiphany's glow shine brightly as we approach the work before us—new ministries, budget adjustments, the election of vestry members, annual meetings, and the many other challenges that inaugurate a new year.

Vestry Discussion

- Have you and your family recognized the Feast of the Epiphany and the weeks that follow in any specific way? If so, how? If not, why not?
- How might this season shape your spiritual journey and prepare you for Lent?
- What does your parish do to mark the Epiphany season beyond the celebration of the feast? Should and could more be done? If so, what?
- As the light of Epiphany breaks into the world, how might your parish break anew into your community?

Something to Ponder

As the title of this reflection suggests, lots get lost in the shuffle of the Epiphany season. The constant, however, is the image of a brilliant star and the path it lights for all who travel to Bethlehem and beyond. You're invited to spend time with the concept of "light" and how it shapes your faith, ministry, and congregational leadership.

Lent's Call: Seeking and Sharing Forgiveness

Opening Prayer

O God, the abundance of whose mercy was made manifest in the gift of his Son, even unto death on the cross: humble us as we unmask and acknowledge lives that daily fall short of your glory; give voice to our confession and our petition for forgiveness; share your grace, which absolves our sins; and send your Spirit to guide our work as we strive to lead the faithful of our parish in the proclamation of the Good News of Jesus Christ in our service to the world. In whose Name we pray. Amen.

A Quote for Your Consideration

As we enter the season of Lent, we're brought to our knees by our own sinfulness, the pain caused by others, and the suffering of the world. So too do we look to Jesus on the cross as He summoned His Father to forgive those who put Him to death. You're invited to consider the following quote from seventeenth-century Anglican priest and poet John Donne as we reflect on the unbounded grace of God's forgiveness and the imperative to share it bountifully as Jesus' disciples (2002c):

> O Lord, thou hast set up many candlesticks, and kindled many lamps in me, but I have either blown them out or carried them to guide me in . . . forbidden ways. Thou hast given me a desire of knowledge, and some means to it, and some possession of it, and I have armed myself with thy weapons against thee. Yet, O God, have mercy upon me, for thine own sake have mercy on me. Let not sin and me be able to exceed thee, nor to defraud thee, nor to frustrate thy purposes: But let me, in despite of me, be of so much use to thy glory, that by thy mercy to my sin, other sinners see how much sin thou canst pardon.

Leadership in Context

Whether on the board of a multinational corporation or an ad hoc group of advisers to a not-for-profit start-up, disagreements emerge, personalities bristle, and heartfelt confrontations occur. Contentious issues may focus on many matters, including, for example, policy and finance, strategic direction, and leadership style. Regardless of the source, however, they all too frequently deteriorate into *ad hominem* attacks, with the participants challenging each other's integrity. Predictably, acrimony increases, positions harden, and little is accomplished—at least in the short-term.

The Church is certainly not immune to internal squabbles nor the hurt, alienation, and schism that often result. Henry VIII's sixteenth-century standoff with Pope Clement VII over the annulment of the king's marriage, the Lutheran Church Missouri Synod's 1970s split regarding matters of Biblical interpretation, doctrine, and pastoral practice, and the struggle between the late Pope Francis and his conservative opponents within the Vatican bureaucracy illustrate the long history of ecclesiastical strife turned personal.

Likewise, individual congregations regularly experience the pain that comes from power struggles within. The ordination of women and those who identify as LGBTQ+, an "open table" for Communion, and the embrace of strategies to enhance diversity, equity, and inclusion, among so many others, have ignited fractious debate within local faith communities. And not unlike the historic Church, the consequences have frequently damaged the Body of Christ—turning friends and family against one another, stifling ministry, and limiting the proclamation of the Gospel.

The early Church found itself mired in just this circumstance, recounted in Acts 15.1–21:

> Then certain individuals came down from Judea and were teaching the brothers, "Unless you are circumcised according to the custom of Moses, you cannot be saved." And after Paul and Barnabas had no small dissension and debate with them, Paul and Barnabas and some of the others were appointed to go up to Jerusalem to discuss this question with the apostles and the elders. So they were sent on their way by the church, and as they passed through both Phoenicia and Samaria, they reported the conversion of the Gentiles, and brought great joy to all the believers. When they came to Jerusalem, they were welcomed by the church and the apostles and the elders, and they reported all that God had done with them. But some believers who belonged to the sect of the Pharisees stood up and said, "It is necessary for them to be circumcised and ordered to keep the law of Moses."
>
> The apostles and the elders met together to consider this matter. After there had been much debate, Peter stood up and said to them, "My brothers, you know that in the early days God made a choice among you, that I should be the one through whom the Gentiles would hear the message of the good news and become believers. And God, who knows the human heart, testified to them by giving them the

Holy Spirit, just as he did to us; and in cleansing their hearts by faith he has made no distinction between them and us. Now, therefore, why are you putting God to the test by placing on the neck of the disciples a yoke that neither our ancestors nor we have been able to bear? On the contrary, we believe that we will be saved through the grace of the Lord Jesus, just as they will." The whole assembly kept silence, and listened to Barnabas and Paul as they told of all the signs and wonders that God had done through them among the Gentiles. After they finished speaking, James replied, "My brothers, listen to me. Simeon has related how God first looked favorably on the Gentiles, to take from among them a people for his name. This agrees with the words of the prophets, as it is written, 'After this I will return, and I will rebuild the dwelling of David, which has fallen; from its ruins I will rebuild it, and I will set it up, so that all other peoples may seek the Lord—even all the Gentiles over whom my name has been called. Thus says the Lord, who has been making these things known from long ago.'" Therefore I have reached the decision that we should not trouble those Gentiles who are turning to God, but we should write to them to abstain only from things polluted by idols and from fornication and from whatever has been strangled and from blood. For in every city, for generations past, Moses has had those who proclaim him, for he has been read aloud every sabbath in the synagogues.

Peter initially argued that followers of Christ must first become Jews by being circumcised and following the Law given in the Torah. However, Paul (himself a faithful Pharisee) insisted that in Christ there is no distinction between Christian and Jew, man or woman, or free person or slave. We have the sense from the text that the exchange of perspectives may have been especially tense.

However rather than digging in his heels, Peter listened intently to Paul's argument, found it persuasive, and then urged his supporters to adopt Paul's more inclusive position. Why? Not because Paul was the more effective debater. But rather because he raised Jesus' own embrace of all whose lives he touched as the model for Christian community.

Although Acts does not report on specific exchanges between Peter and Paul, it seems clear from the outcome of their testy and quite personal debate that they found common ground rooted in mutual understanding, forgiveness, and reconciliation. Their journey together and the restoration of their relationship seem to exemplify the work to which we're called and the way we resolve conflict. As with Peter and Paul, we look to Jesus as the model for understanding differences, accepting each other as equally valued children of God, and focusing our ministry on the Good News of salvation through Jesus Christ.

Vestry Discussion

- How do challenges, shortcomings, frustrations, and failures affect your life and ability to lead your congregation as a member of the vestry?

- What have you learned about the grace of God's forgiveness that has shaped your life and the leadership of your congregation?
- What might your vestry do to model self-forgiveness and the forgiveness of others for your parish?

Something to Ponder

Although essential to personal piety, forgiveness also functions as a critical element of our work together as members of the vestry. Even as our disagreements occasionally spawn pain and anger, we're called by our Lord to forgive and reconcile with one another. Therefore, you're invited to reflect on "forgiveness and reconciliation" as you consider how individually and collectively they might shape your ministry.

Easter's Challenge

Opening Prayer

Lord Christ, we rejoice in your victory over death and resurrection, your enduring presence in the bread and wine of Eucharist, and your unfailing promise to be with us throughout all eternity. As we bask in your light and begin to absorb fully the meaning of your triumph, grow our belief; clear our confusion and doubt; nurture our prayers; and enable us to envision who we are to be as your faithful people. For your mercy's sake. Amen.

A Quote for Your Consideration

Easter and its immediate aftermath present a particularly challenging conundrum. On the one hand, we're to rejoice in Jesus' conquest of death and His resurrection. On the other, we're left with no instructions and no specific plan for the future. Like His disciples, we find ourselves wondering, sometimes confused, and trying to grasp the import of what we've just experienced. Nineteenth-century Anglican theologian and leader of the Oxford Movement Edward Pusey puts this awkward time in context (2002):

> And what then on this "our triumphant Holy Day," should His Life be? What but the Sealing to us of all which He had wrought for us? What of the bursting of the bars of our prison-house, the restoration, of our lost Paradise, the opening of the Kingdom of Heaven, the earnest of our Endless Life, the binding of the strong man, and letting us, his lawful prisoners, free, the bringing in of Incorruption, the Conquest, in the Head, of the last enemy, that he may, one by one, be conquered in us too, and the death of our bodies may be the deliverance from "this body of death," our souls' perfected life? Can there be more than this? There can.

Leadership in Context

Each year, the events of Holy Week leave us reeling. We begin with Jesus' followers welcoming him to Jerusalem with a joyful parade—a marked contrast to the fear instilled by

Roman Governor Pontius Pilate's entrance with his soldiers the same day. But with breathtaking speed, the scene deteriorates. Jesus throws money changers out of the Temple. He gathers his disciples for a last meal together and then leads them to Gethsemane for prayer where he's betrayed and taken into custody. Convicted, sentenced to death, crucified, buried, and resurrected—all in just a week!

> After the sabbath, as the first day of the week was dawning, Mary Magdeline and the other Mary went to see the tomb. And suddenly there was a great earthquake; for an angel of the Lord, descending from heaven, came and rolled back the stone and sat on it. His appearance was like lightning, and his clothing white as snow. For fear of him the guards shook and became like dead men. But the angel said to the women, "Do not be afraid; I know that you are looking for Jesus who was crucified. He is not here; for he has been raised, as he said. Come, see the place where he lay. Then go quickly and tell his disciples, 'He has been raised from the dead, and indeed he is going ahead of you to Galilee; there you will see him'" (Matthew 28.1–7a).

Later that day, an angel invited the disciples to return with Jesus to their homeland in Galilee so that they might see him. We're not provided with any of the details of what they were thinking and doing in the three days since Jesus died, nor do we know what his expectation of them was once they arrived in Galilee.

John gives us a bit more information about the disciples' state of mind immediately following the crucifixion. "When it was evening on that day, the first day of the week, and the doors of the house where the disciples had met were locked for fear of the Jews" (20.19a). We also learn that they received the gift of the Holy Spirit and the charge to grant absolution of sins ... and to withhold it. As in John's narrative, the disciples spend time with Jesus on the shores of the "Sea of Tiberius" (Sea of Galilee). Yet again, however, they receive little direction other than to, "Feed my sheep" (John 21.17).

Relating several post-resurrection encounters, Luke (24.13–49) focuses on Jesus' invitation to believe. Important, to be sure, but hardly a roadmap to answer our questions or connect the discipleship dots. Mark in his usual sparse and abrupt rhetoric recounts only that Jesus sent his disciples to proclaim, "the sacred and imperishable proclamation of eternal salvation" (Mark 16.9 Shorter Ending).

What's clear is that Jesus' disciples were hunkered down, afraid, and even when they encountered him had, at best, only minimal direction for the lives they were to live. We find our Easter selves in the same place: startled by an empty tomb, amazed by a resurrection, and wondering what to do.

It's easy to fast-forward to Pentecost when we'll share in the Holy Spirit's gift to Jesus' faithful and begin to explore the depths of discipleship. But the reality is we live these next 50 days wondering what to do. Hide? Pray? Retreat to a lake, the mountains, or the desert?

Just as the disciples must have been stumped by the future they're to engage, so too are we challenged individually and as congregational leaders by the vagaries of Easter's aftermath.

To be sure, we share with the clergy the responsibility for celebrating and proclaiming resurrection's joy. But it's also a time to pause and allow its full impact to work on our hearts and souls.

The events of Holy Week were traumatic for the disciples, as well as us. And resurrection, while changing the cosmos forever, is an experience that must be lived into. It must be given time to envelop us and overcome our pain and doubts. We need time for intentional reflection and prayer as we consider resurrection's expectations for our lives. And we are consciously to prepare ourselves to receive Pentecost's Holy Spirit and embark on the proclamation of the Good News of Christ risen and the ministry to which we've been called.

So, what to do in these Great 50 Days of Easter? Bask in the light of an empty tomb. Internalize resurrection's saving grace through reflection and prayer. Anticipate with joy and hope what's to come. And remember that resurrection is not the end of our journey of faith. In response to Edward Pusey's earlier question, "Can there be more than this?" We join with him in responding, "There can."

Vestry Discussion

- How has your understanding of Eastertide and the spiritual discipline it entails changed over time?
- In partnership with the clergy, what might the vestry do to encourage a deeper exploration of "resurrection" within your parish?
- How might the resurrection narrative shape your congregation's ministry in the larger community?

- How can we purposefully use the Great 50 Days of Easter to prepare for Pentecost?

Something to Ponder

The season of Easter is rich with opportunities to mine the many dimensions of resurrection in our individual lives, the life of the Church, and the life of the world. It's also a time to lay the foundation for what we're to do as a "resurrection community," a concept you're invited to consider as we lead our congregation through these Great 50 Days.

The Voice of Pentecost

Opening Prayer

God of infinite presence, whose Spirit dwells in our hearts and guides our ministry among the privileged and marginalized alike: open our eyes to see the pain, needs, and anger of the world; enable us to embrace hope for the future for which your people long; help us discern how best to serve as the instruments of your *shalom*; and provide us with the strength and patience to persevere. In the Name of the Father, Son and Holy Spirit. Amen.

A Quote for Your Consideration

Annually, we rejoice in Pentecost's celebration and the beginning of a lengthy season of exploring Jesus' ministry and the invitation to join Him. The challenges are many, but at their core is the gift of God's Spirit who forever changes our lives, our perspective on the world around us, and the urgency with which we're summoned to act. As we prepare to engage this "Ordinary Time," you're invited to consider the following quote from nineteenth-century Dean of St. Paul's Cathedral in London, Richard William Church (2003):

> Pentecost is the commemoration of the birthday of the new birth of Humanity itself; of the day when a new divine power came into the very inmost souls and beings of men, changing them from their old selves, filling them with new energies fresh from the very heart of God, begetting them anew from the deadness of sin, giving them, by a new birth through the Spirit, the power to become the sons of God.

Leadership in Context

Unlike the other principal feasts of the Church, Pentecost poses distinct ambiguity and, while there is a symbol of the season (a dove), what the faithful are specifically to do in response often seems elusive. The scene at Bethlehem's manger, for example, symbolizes the Divine breaking into the world and summons us to imagine the impact of God's gift to humanity during the 12 days of Christmastide. Similarly, Easter is marked by an empty tomb and 50 days basking in the light of Jesus' victory over death and the assurance of life eternal. But while a dove commemorates the Spirit sent to dwell among us on Pentecost, how we live with and into it during the months of Ordinary Time that follow can be difficult to grasp—so many expectations, so many options, so many challenges. To be sure, we're to learn from Jesus' ministry and model ours after his. We're to grow in faith. And we're to mature as followers of "the Way." But what does that mean especially for the vestry—the lay leaders of the congregation?

The events of the first Pentecost (Acts 2.12) provide us with context, if not specific direction:

> When the day of Pentecost had come, they were all together in one place. And suddenly from heaven there came a sound like the rush of a violent wind, and it filled the entire house where they were sitting. Divided tongues, as of fire, appeared among them, and a tongue rested on each of them. All of them were filled with the Holy Spirit and began to speak in other languages, as the Spirit gave them ability.
>
> Now there were devout Jews from every people under heaven living in Jerusalem. And at this sound the crowd gathered and was bewildered, because each one heard them speaking in the native language of each. Amazed and astonished, they asked, "Are not all these who are speaking Galileans? And how is it that we hear, each of us, in our own native language? Parthians, Medes, Elamites, and residents of Mesopotamia, Judea and Cappadocia, Pontus and Asia, Phrygia and Pamphylia, Egypt and the parts of Libya belonging to Cyrene, and visitors from Rome, both Jews and proselytes, Cretans and Arabs—in our own languages we hear them speaking about God's deeds of power." All were amazed and perplexed, saying to one another, "What does this mean?"

The strange events of Pentecost have sparked speculation for millennia. Was the "violent wind" merely the passing of a weather front that happened to coincide with the gathering? And, what about the "tongues of fire"—let alone split above the heads of the onlookers? Perhaps most intriguing, however, has been the debate about the cacophony that erupted among the crowd. Many in the charismatic movement have argued for the concept of *glossolalia*—unintelligible speech brought about by the presence of the Holy Spirit. However, the languages of Pentecost were well known to the many different nationalities represented in Jerusalem that day. Rather than an inexplicable miracle, Pentecost reminds us of God's intent to meet each of us uniquely, exactly where we are—to hear our distinct concerns, to understand our specific needs, and to speak to each of us in a way we can understand. But it also calls into question what this gift means for the collective Body of Christ, the Church. How and where do we find common ground as God speaks to us in our own tongues?

Each of us within this community has a distinct narrative that describes our faith journey and sets forth our hopes, expectations, and sometimes our fears for life within our congregational family. The challenge for clergy and lay members alike is to listen carefully to these stories, acknowledge their truth, and respond with understanding and grace. Our prayerful hope is that our mutual ministry regularly touches everyone with the Good News of the Gospel, knowing that some expectations unfortunately will not or cannot be met.

But as important as embracing the chronicles of our respective lives is, a congregation is more than the sum of its stories. It has a distinct communal pulse, unique rhythm, and defined ethos that embody the collective presence and work of the parish as a single entity. From this perspective, Pentecost invites the clergy and vestry to look beyond our individual experiences—our own voices—toward the integrated voice we share with the world around us. How, for example, do we position our congregation in relation to the needs of the larger community? What are we known for (if anything)? What impact have we had on the lives of those within our midst and beyond? Who would miss us if we closed our doors?

To be sure, we'll explore the multifaceted dimensions of Christian discipleship throughout the Season of Pentecost—learning from Jesus' example and applying it not only individually but using it also to shape the identity of our congregation so that we speak with a voice the world understands. We have much to do!

Vestry Discussion

- What is "the voice" of your congregation?
- How is this voice known and received by the larger community?
- What can the vestry do to facilitate a common understanding of "our voice"?

Something to Ponder

Pentecost challenges us to reconcile our "individual voices" with the "collective" as we fashion our parish's ministry. Reflecting on both, you're invited to consider "common purpose" in the context of the presence we hope to be in our community.

Creation: Celebration and Care

Opening Prayer

Almighty God, who from nothing birthed all creation: forgive the selfish appropriation of your gifts for our purposes rather than yours; pardon the harm we continue to cause to the world we inhabit; bring us into a just and loving relationship with all that surrounds us; grant us the humility and wisdom to serve as partners in the stewardship of creation; and empower our voice as we work for justice, equity, and sustainability. In Jesus' Name and for the sake of the world, we pray. Amen.

A Quote for Your Consideration

The Church's distinct calendar has long served to mark the liturgical seasons we engage in worship: Advent, Christmas, Epiphany, Lent, Easter, and Pentecost. Each has a specific focus that provides insight into the nature of God. For example, Advent highlights our hope and expectation for the long-promised Messiah, while Easter summons us to enter the life of the risen Christ. In 1989, Ecumenical Patriarch Dimitrios I declared September 1 as a day of prayer for creation amid the season of Pentecost, followed by the World Council of Churches' subsequent extension of the creation care theme through October 4, the Feast of St. Francis of Assisi.

Despite the environmental progress since the late Senator Gaylord Nelson's inauguration of "Earth Day" in the spring of 1970, the world community finds itself in a precarious position, with unprecedented assaults on virtually every dimension of creation. Individually, we often are overwhelmed by the complexity of the challenges posed by a planet experiencing such profound changes. And collectively, rampant partisanship fueled by science skepticism has hobbled and frequently halted the ability to marshal this country's vast intellectual and financial resources in addressing key environmental issues.

Certainly, there are many explanations for political indecisiveness, policy confusion, and inconsistent action. Especially intriguing, however, is the observation offered by philosopher and activist Bayo Akomolafe (2024):

> Everywhere I was invited to speak, I offered an invitation to "slow down," which seems like the wrong thing to do when there's fire on the mountain. But here's the point: in "hurrying up" all the time, we often lose sight of the abundance of resources that might help us meet today's most challenging crises. We rush through into the same patterns we are used to. Of course, there isn't a single way to respond to crisis; there is no universally correct way. However, the call to slow down works to bring us face to face with the invisible, the hidden, the unremarked, the yet-to-be-resolved. Sometimes, what is the appropriate thing to do is not the effective thing to do.
>
> Slowing down is thus about lingering in the places we are not used to. Seeking out new questions. Becoming accountable to more than what rests on the surface. Seeking roots. Slowing down is taking care of ghosts, hugging monsters, sharing silence, embracing the weird.

Leadership in Context

The challenges to creation are many and often seem insurmountable—a climate in crisis, the search for carbon-neutral energy, the sustainability of agriculture, and rising sea levels, to name only a few. But it's in the face of this broad array of urgent issues that Akomolafe encourages a deliberate, disciplined, and patient approach to considering specific problems, the options available to address them, and the subtleties embedded in both. Implicit is also the need for the application of a consistent framework for evaluation, policy formulation, and strategic implementation in our own communities and around the world.

In partnership with the Earth Bible Project, Lutheran Biblical scholar and theologian Rev. Dr. Norman Habel has proposed several principles to guide the care of creation (Season of Creation: A Guide for episcopal Parishes, 2024). Paramount is the inherent value of each individual element of God's creation. So too are they interconnected and dependent on each other for their sustenance. The principle of "voice" acknowledges that creation is a living organism able to advocate for a just response to its needs. Additionally, we're to understand that the universe and its infinite elements have a specific purpose in the structure and functioning of the cosmos. The fifth principle asserts that humans are partners with (not rulers over) creation and are charged to ensure its diversity and sustainability. Finally, resistance to injustice is incumbent on all of creation.

As fundamental as these principles are, the author of the Book of Revelation reminds us that their purpose is to shape human action in a way that recognizes that all creation serves to glorify the God who ordered it, declaring, "You are worthy, our Lord and God, to receive glory and honor and power, for you created all things, and by your will they existed and were created" (Revelation 4.11). In the individual stewardship of our small slice of the world, the decisions we make as congregational leaders or the policies we embrace in the political arena, the temptation is all too present to ground them in what we find most personally gratifying. Revelation's rejoinder is an invitation to celebrate God's ongoing creative enterprise, as well as subordinate our individual preferences to the common good envisioned in creation. But how?

A process that might guide our deliberations and transform the principles of creation care articulated by Habel into actionable strategies has been advanced by Episcopal priest and climate activist Rev. Dr. Margaret Bullitt-Jonas (Season of Creation: A Guide for Episcopal Parishes, 2024). It rightfully begins by opening ourselves to a conversation with God in prayer—voicing our concerns, raising our petitions, and listening intently. Especially at a time of climate change denial and "alternate facts," research and education are essential to understanding the environmental challenges we encounter and the fact-based and responsible alternatives for solving them. However, even the most incisive empirical research and good intentions are not sufficient to address these issues. Action—intentional, focused, and principled—is required to initiate and sustain progress in our work to reclaim creation from the damage humans have and continue to cause. And finally, Bullitt-Jonas summons us to corporate boardrooms, the public square, and the halls of government to advocate policies that protect creation and make its gifts accessible to all. To her four-fold typology, others have recently added the critical liturgical act of blessing, imploring God to direct our ministry and approve the work of our hands even as we rejoice in the work of God's (2024).

Clergy and vestries play a pivotal role in leading responsible creation care initiatives within their congregations and larger communities. Individually, we model environmental stewardship through our own behavior—the cars we drive, the source of energy we use to cook and heat our homes, the way we landscape and care for our yards, and the many other decisions we make that impact our planet. Organizationally, we have the opportunity to use the congregation's resources to improve the sustainability of our facilities and grounds. And as members of the Church Universal, we can actively support and pursue policies that preserve the treasured inheritance of the universe and the earth we inhabit. In doing so, we're reminded in the words of the Episcopal Hymn #416 (1982), "For the Beauty of the Earth," of the purpose of our work:

> For each perfect gift of thine
> > to the world so freely given,
> faith and hope and love divine,
> > peace on earth and joy in heaven
> Christ our God,
> > to thee we raise
> this our hymn
> > of grateful praise.

Vestry Discussion

- How do you interpret your Christian discipleship and vestry leadership in the context of the care of creation?
- What are the creation care priorities for you and your household? Why?
- What are the creation care priorities for your congregation? Why?
- What are the impediments to the care of creation that you encounter in your personal, congregational, and professional life? How might they be overcome?

Something to Ponder

The care of creation is a daily test requiring our faithful stewardship, innovation, and resolve. It also necessitates a commitment to the common good. In considering this formidable personal, congregational, and social challenge, you're invited to reflect on "perseverance" as an essential element of your ministry.

CLOSING PRAYER

The reflections included in this book were prepared for a vestry that regularly meets in the evening. Certainly, there are many resources available for prayers to conclude a meeting or stimulate extemporaneous prayer focused on the specific issues addressed in it. I've found the following prayer, inspired by and adapted from the *New Zealand Prayer Book's* "Night Prayer" (1989), to be especially inviting:

> *Lord, as night now envelops us, let us put aside the cares of day and rest in the presence of God. "What has been done is done. What has not been done has not been done. Let it be." Grant us peaceful sleep, the dreams of possibilities beyond our imaginations and the joy of awaking to the dawn of a new day filled with hope, joy and God's love for all whose lives we might touch. Amen.*

REFERENCES

"Alleluia, Sing to Jesus." 1982. *The Hymnal 1982*, 460. New York: Church Publishing Incorporated.

Akomolafe, Bayo. 2024. "A Slower Urgency." https://www.bayoakomolafe.net/post/a-slower-urgency.

Avis, Paul. 2000. "Ministry." In *The Oxford Companion to Christian Thought: Intellectual, Spiritual and Moral Horizons of Christianity*, edited by Adrian Hastings, Alistair Mason, and Hugh Pyper, 437–38. New York: Oxford University Press.

Barth, Karl. 2004. *Church Dogmatics: The Doctrine of Reconciliation*. London: T. & T. Clark, 41–2.

"Be Thou My Vision." ca. 700. Versified by Mary Elizabeth Byrne and Translated by Eleanor Hull and Adapted from *The Church Hymnary*, 1927. In *The Hymnal 1982*, 488. New York: Church Publishing Incorporated.

Boring, M. Eugene. 1995. "Gospel of Matthew." In *The New Interpreter's Bible*, edited by Leander E. Keck et al., 89–505. Nashville: Abingdon Press.

Centers for Disease Control. *Suicide Data and Statistics*. 2024. Atlanta: Centers for Disease Control.

"Christ is Made the Sure Foundation." ca. 600. Translated in *Hymns Ancient and Modern*, 1861 after John Mason Neale. Music by Henry Purcell, adapted by James Gillespie. *The Hymnal 1982*, 518. New York: Church Publishing Incorporated.

Church, Richard William. 2003. "The Imperfections of Religious Believers." In *Love's Redeeming Work: The Anglican Quest for Holiness*, edited by Geoffrey Rowell, Kenneth Stevenson, and Rowan Williams, 441–2. Oxford: Oxford University Press.

"Come, Gracious Spirit, Heavenly Dove." Simon Browne. Melody from the *Methodist Harmonist*, 1821, adapted by Lowell Mason. *The Hymnal 1982*, 512. New York: Church Publishing Incorporated.

"Come Thou Font of Every Blessing." Words by Robert Robinson. Melody from *A Repository of Sacred Music, Part II*, 1813. *The Hymnal 1982*, 686. New York: Church Publishing Incorporated.

Dix, Dom Gregory. 2005. *The Shape of the Liturgy*, 3rd ed. New York: Continuum, xviii.

Donne, John. 2002a. "The Bell Tolls." In *Glorious Companions: Five Centuries of Anglican Spirituality*, by Richard H. Schmidt, 56. Grand Rapids, MI: William B. Eerdmans Publishing Company.

Donne, John. 2002b. "The Coming of God." In *Glorious Companions: Five Centuries of Anglican Spirituality*, by Richard H. Schmidt, 52. Grand Rapids, MI: William B. Eerdmans Publishing Company.

Donne, John. 2002c. "Prayer for Forgiveness." In *Glorious Companions: Five Centuries of Anglican Spirituality*, by Richard H. Schmidt, 51–2. Grand Rapids, MI: William B. Eerdmans Publishing Company.

Dozier, Verna J. 2002. "The Church's Business." In *Glorious Companions: Five Centuries of Anglican Spirituality*, by

Richard H. Schmidt, 292. Grand Rapids, MI: William B. Eerdmans Publishing Company.

Eva, N., Robin, M., Sendjaya, S., Dierendonck, D., and Liden, R.C. 2019. "Servant Leadership: A Systematic Review and Call for Future Research." *The Leadership Quarterly* 30 (1): 111–32.

"For the Beauty of the Earth." 1982. *The Hymnal 1982*, 416. New York: Church Publishing Incorporated.

Giles, Richard. 2004. *Re-Pitching the Tent: The Definitive Guide to Re-Ordering Church Buildings for Worship and Mission*, 3rd ed. Norwich, England: Canterbury Press.

Gore, Charles. 2002. "Authority." In *Glorious Companions: Five Centuries of Anglican Spirituality*, by Richard H. Schmidt, 212. Grand Rapids, MI: William B. Eerdmans Publishing Company.

Gortner, David. 2008. *Transforming Evangelism*. New York: Church Publishing, 1, 3, 25, 29.

Gray, Donald. 2000. "Worship." In *The Oxford Companion to Christian Thought: Intellectual, Spiritual, and Moral Horizons of Christianity*, edited by Adrian Hastings, Alistair Mason, and Hugh Pyper, 763. Oxford: Oxford University Press.

Greenleaf, R. 1983. *Servant Leadership: A Journey into the Nature of Legitimate Power and Greatness*. Mahwah, New Jersey: Paulist Press.

Harries, Richard. 2024. *Wounded I Sing: From Advent to Christmas with George Herbert*. London: SPCK, 48.

Hauerwas, Stanley, and Charles Pinches. 2001. "Courage Exemplified." *The Hauerwas Reader*, edited by John

Berkman and Michael Cartwright, 291, Durham, NC: Duke University Press.

Heitzenrater, R.P. 1995. *Wesley and the People Called Methodists*. Nashville, TN: Abingdon Press, 80.

Hooker, Richard. 2002. "Holy Communion." In *Glorious Companions: Five Centuries of Anglican Spirituality*, by Richard H. Schmidt, 31. Grand Rapids, MI: William B. Eerdmans Publishing Company.

"How Lovely Is Thy Dwelling Place." Paraphrase of Psalm 84, stanzas 1–2, In *The Psalms of David in Meeter, 1650* and stanzas 3–4 by Carl P. Daw, Jr. Music by J. L. Macbeth Bain. In *The Hymnal 1982*, 517. New York: Church Publishing Incorporated.

"I Come with Joy to Meet My Lord." Words by Brian A. Wren. Music adapted from *Land of Rest* and harmonized by Annabel Morris Buchanan. Words copyright 1971 by Hope Publishing Company. In *The Hymnal 1982*, 304. New York: Church Publishing Incorporated.

"I Want to Walk as a Child of the Light." Words and Music copyright 1970 and 1975 by Celebration. In *The Hymnal 1982*, 490. New York: Church Publishing Incorporated.

Johnson, Samuel. 2002. "Words and Actions." In *Glorious Companions: Five Centuries of Anglican Spirituality*, by Richard H. Schmidt 147. Grand Rapids, MI: William B. Eerdmans Publishing Company.

Kavanagh, Aidan. 1984. *On Liturgical Theology*. Collegeville, MN: The Liturgical Press, 91–2.

Kelley, Melissa M. 2010. *Grief: Contemporary Theory and the Practice of Ministry*. Minneapolis, MN: Fortress Press.

Kivengere, Festo. 2002. "Reconciliation." In Richard H. Schmidt's *Glorious Companions: Five Centuries of Anglican Spirituality*, 317. Grand Rapids, MI: William B. Eerdmans Publishing Company.

Kubler-Ross, E. 2014. *On Death and Dying: What the Dying Have to Teach, Doctors, Nurses, Clergy and Their Own Families*. New York: Scribner.

Law, William. 2002. "Fiscal Madness." In *Glorious Companions: Five Centuries of Anglican Spirituality*, by Richard H. Schmidt, 101. Grand Rapids, MI: William B. Eerdmans Publishing Company.

L'Engle, Madelein. 2002. "How to Spot a True Christian." In *Glorious Companions: Five Centuries of Anglican Spirituality*, by Richard H. Schmidt, 08. Grand Rapids, MI: William B. Eerdmans Publishing Company.

Long, Kimberly Bracken. 2008. "Homiletical Perspective on John 1.1-14." In *Feasting on the Word: Preaching the Revised Common Lectionary, Year B, Volume 1*, edited by David L. Bartlett and Barbara Taylor Brown, 140–5. Knoxville, TN: Westminster John Knox Press.

Lupton, Robert D. 2011. *Toxic Charity: How Churches and Charities Hurt Those They Help (And How to Reverse It)*. New York: HarperOne.

Maurice, Frederick D. 2002a. "Do Not Praise the Liturgy." In Richard H. Schmidt's *Glorious Companions: Five Centuries of Anglican Spirituality*, 194. Grand Rapids, MI: William B. Eerdmans Publishing Company.

Maurice, Frederick D. 2002b. "Dogmatism." In *Glorious Companions: Five Centuries of Anglican Spirituality*, by

Richard H. Schmidt, 191. Grand Rapids, MI: William B. Eerdmans Publishing Company.

McIntosh, Mark A. 2004. *Discernment and Truth: The Spirituality and Theology of Knowledge*. New York: Herder & Herder, 8–22, 19.

McMichael, Ralph. 2019. *The Eucharistic Faith*. London: SCM Press, 247.

Merton, Thomas. 2007. *New Seeds of Contemplation*. New York: New Directions Publishing Corporation, 98.

Miller, Charles. 1995. *Praying the Eucharist: Reflections on the Eucharistic Experience of God*. Harrisburg, PA: Morehouse Publishing.

More, Hannah. 2002. "Prayer." In *Glorious Companions: Five Centuries of Anglican Spirituality*, by Richard H. Schmidt, 161. Grand Rapids, MI: William B. Eerdmans Publishing Company.

Nouwen, Henri J. M. 1977. *The Living Reminder: Service and Prayer in Memory of Jesus Christ*. San Francisco: HarperSanFrancisco, 48.

Pavelsky, Robert L. 2005. "Crisis Intervention Theory." In *Dictionary of Pastoral Care and Counseling*, edited by Rodney J. Hunter, 245–6. Nashville, TN: Abingdon Press.

Pilch, John J. 2003. "Serve, Servant, Service." In *The Westminster Theological Wordbook of the Bible*, edited by Donald E. Gowan, 459–62. Louisville, KY: Westminster John Knox Press.

Pinker, Steven. 2012. *The Better Angels of Our Nature: Why Violence Has Declined*. New York: Penguin.

Pruyser, Paul W. 2005. "Hope and Despair." *Dictionary of Pastoral Care and Counseling*, edited by Rodney J. Hunter, 532–4. Nashville, TN: Abingdon Press.

Price, Charles P. and Louis Weil. 2000. *Liturgy for Living*, rev. ed. Harrisburg, PA: Morehouse Publishing, 14, 25–33.

Pusey, Edward. 2002. "Deification: The Easter life of Christians in Christ." In *Love's Redeeming Work: The Anglican Quest for Holiness*, edited by Geoffrey Rowell, Kenneth Stevenson, and Rowan Williams, 398. Oxford: Oxford University Press.

Robinson, John A. T. 2001. "Learning from Cancer." In *Love's Redeeming Work: The Anglican Quest for Holiness*, edited by Geoffrey Rowell, Kenneth Stevenson, and Rowan Williams, 727. Oxford: Oxford University Press.

Saint Benedict's Rule. 1997. York, England: Ampleforth Abbey Press, 10.

Sandys, E. 2002. "Fear and Love." In *Love's Redeeming Work: The Anglican Quest for Holiness*, edited by Geoffrey Rowell, Kenneth Stevenson, and Rowan Williams, 64. Oxford: Oxford University Press.

Season of Creation: A Celebration Guide for Episcopal Parishes. 2024. New York: The Episcopal Church.

Shanks, Andrew. 2000. "Peace." In *The Oxford Companion to Christian Thought: Intellectual, Spiritual, and Moral Horizons of Christianity*, edited by Adrian Hastings, Alistair Mason, and Hugh Pyper, 763, Oxford: Oxford University Press.

Sharkey, Patrick. 2018. *Uneasy Peace: The Great Crime Decline, the Renewal of City Life, and the Next War on Violence*. New York: W. W. Norton & Company.

Smith, Marc D. 2020. *Each Other's Keeper: The Church's Response to Violence*. Cincinnati, OH: Forward Movement's ChurchNext and St. Louis, MO: Episcopal Diocese of Missouri.

Taylor, Barbara Brown. 1998. "Magnificat." In *Mixed Blessings*. Lanham, Maryland: Cowley Publications, 36.

Taylor, Jeremy. 2002. "Prayer for a Contented Spirit." In *Glorious Companions: Five Centuries of Anglican Spirituality*, by Richard H. Schmidt, 78. Grand Rapids, MI: William B. Eerdmans Publishing Company.

Temple, William. 2002a. "Charity as Blood Money." In *Glorious Companions: Five Centuries of Anglican Spirituality*, by Richard H. Schmidt, 263. Grand Rapids, MI: William B. Eerdmans Publishing Company.

Temple, William. 2002b. "The Darkness and the Light." In *Glorious Companions: Five Centuries of Anglican Spirituality*, by Richard H. Schmidt, 261. Grand Rapids, MI: William B. Eerdmans Publishing Company.

The Book of Common Prayer. 1979. New York: Oxford University Press, 383, 568, 827, 845–878.

The New Zealand Prayer Book. 1989. San Francisco: HarperSanFrancisco, 184.

"Thou Whose Almighty Word." Words by John Marriott. Music by Felice de Giardini and harmonized in *The New Hymnal*, 1916, based on *Hymns Ancient and Modern*, 1875, and Lowell Mason. In *The Hymnal 1982*, 371. New York: Church Publishing Incorporated.

Wesley, John. "Regeneration." 2002. In *Glorious Companions: Five Centuries of Anglican Spirituality*, by Richard H.

Schmidt, 120. Grand Rapids, MI: William B. Eerdmans Publishing Company.

White, Susan J. 2002. "Can We Talk About a Theology of Sacred Space?" *Searching for Sacred Space: Essays on Architecture and Liturgical Design in the Episcopal Church*, edited by John Ander Runkle, 23. New York: Church Publishing Incorporated.

ACKNOWLEDGMENTS

In addition to those who have so graciously offered endorsements and the faith companions to whom this book is dedicated, there are several others who have not only profoundly shaped my life but also whose encouragement and patience over the many decades I've known them have made this book possible. The late Rev. Dr. Carl Graesser, who instilled a love of theology and writing. Dr. Alan Robson, who not only is among my dearest friends and an inspiring mentor but also instilled the values of research discipline and integrity. The Rev. Dr. Barry Hong, my seminary friend and research partner for decades. The late Dr. Virginia Weldon, who "took me under her wing" as an aspiring organizational strategist. Fred Brown, whose health-care leadership most shaped mine (and got me out of any number of jams). And the Rt. Rev. George Wayne Smith, who saw something in my potential for priestly ministry that I could not even imagine.

The list of those to whom I'm deeply indebted for the content and structure of this book include the Bishop's Committee of Ascension Episcopal Church (now All Saints Ascension) in Northwoods, Missouri; the vestry of St. John's Episcopal Church in Boulder, Colorado; editor extraordinaire at Church Publishing Incorporated, Roma Maitlall; and my most treasured critic and beloved wife, Debbie Schuster. While rejoicing in their impact on my life, ministry, and scholarship, any "sins of omission or commission" are mine alone.

www.ingramcontent.com/pod-product-compliance
Lightning Source LLC
Chambersburg PA
CBHW070550160426
43199CB00014B/2438